Women, Reading, Kroetsch

Telling the Difference

SUSAN RUDY DORSCHT

Women, Reading, Kroetsch: Telling the Difference is a book of both practical and theoretical criticism. Some chapters are feminist deconstructive readings of a broad range of the writings of contemporary Canadian poet-critic-novelist Robert Kroetsch, from *But We Are Exiles* to *Completed Field Notes*. Other chapters self-consciously examine the history and possibility of feminist deconstruction and feminist readings of Kroetsch's writing by analyzing Kroetsch, Derrida, and Freud on subjectivity and sexuality; Neuman, Hutcheon, and van Herk on Kroetsch. As such, the book speaks out of and about a number of contemporary theoretical discourses, including particular positions within Canadian literary criticism, feminism, postmodernism, and poststructuralism. Written by a woman reader whose theoretical and methodological orientations are both feminist and poststructuralist, *Women, Reading, Kroetsch: Telling the Difference* problematizes notions of writing, reading, gender, sexuality, and subjectivity in and through Robert Kroetsch's writings. In this critical study of one writer's work the author also challenges the traditionally subservient relationship of reader to text and so empowers the feminist reader as well as, if not rather than, the male writer.

Susan Rudy Dorscht teaches literary and feminist theory, writing by women, and Canadian writings in the English Department at the University of Calgary.

Women, Reading, Kroetsch

Telling the Difference

Women, Reading, Kroetsch

TELLING THE DIFFERENCE

SUSAN RUDY DORSCHT

Wilfrid Laurier University Press

WLU

Canadian Cataloguing in Publication Data

Rudy Dorscht, Susan Arlene, 1961-
Women, Reading, Kroetsch
Includes bibliographical references and index.
ISBN 0-88920-205-2

1. Kroetsch, Robert, 1927- – Criticism and interpretation. 2. Feminist literary criticism. 3. Feminism and literature. I. Title.

PS8521.R64Z85 1991 C813'.54 C91-095476-3
PR9199.3.K76Z85 1991

Cover design by Connolly Art & Design

Printed in Canada

for
Brian,
and for
Erin and Julian

Contents

Acknowledgements

For generous permission to quote from his work and to parody the cover of his book *The Lovely Treachery of Words*, I thank Robert Kroetsch. For permission to re(f)use the photograph which originally appeared on *The Lovely Treachery of Words* and which appears, in altered form, on the cover of this book, I thank Michael Ondaatje. Thanks also to David Garneau for help in reconfiguring the women and Kroetsch on the cover and to Maura Brown for her careful copy-editing.

For academic guidance, intellectual rigour, and emotional support of various kinds I thank Peter Erb, Gary Waller, Barry Cameron, Jamie Dopp, Robert Gibbs, Eli Mandel, Ian Sowton, Barbara Godard, Frank Davey, Shirley Neuman, Jeanne Perreault, Susan Bennett, Tracy Davis, Pauline Butling, Fred Wah, Aritha van Herk, Sandra Woolfrey, Murray McGillivray, Ashraf Rushdy, and Eric Savoy.

Parts of this book have previously appeared in print. Portions of the Introduction and Chapter One appeared in *Open Letter* 7.8 (1990). Earlier versions of Chapters Five and Seven appeared in *Canadian Literature* 119 (1988) and *Open Letter* 6.8 (1987). Chapter Eight appeared in *Signature: A Journal of Theory and Canadian Literature* 2 (1989).

This book has been published with the help of a grant from the Canadian Federation for the Humanities, using funds provided by the Social Sciences and Humanities Research Council of Canada. Without the support of SSHRCC doctoral fellowships from 1985-1988 this book would never have been written.

Finally, for their unflinching confidence in me and their love, I thank my parents, Dorene and Elvin Rudy. For their changing and yet continuing presences, I thank the three people with whom I live, my husband, Brian Dorscht, and our two daughters, Erin and Julian, to whom this book is, out of great love, dedicated.

tell[1] v. (told *pr.* to-)
1. *v.t.* give detailed account of (*as*) in spoken or written words [italics added].
2. make known, divulge, state, express in words, announce openly, assert emphatically.
3. utter.
4. *v.i.* give information or description (*of* or *about*); reveal a secret; inform against (person).
5. *v.t. & i.* decide, determine; *you never can tell*, appearances and probabilities are deceptive.
6. distinguish; *cannot tell them apart, him from his brother.*
7. assure; *it is not easy, I can tell you*; cf. sense 2.
8. *v.i.* produce marked effect; *every blow tells*; have influence in *favour* of or *against*.
9. *v.t.* count; *we were 18 men all told*; reprimand, scold (person).
10. direct, order (person) to do something; *tell him to wait for me.*

—*The Concise Oxford Dictionary*

the *a. & adv.*
1. *a.* (called the *definite article*; placed before *ns.* to denote person[s] or things[s]) already mentioned or under discussion, or from the nature of the case actually or potentially existent, or unique or otherwise sufficiently identified.

—*The Concise Oxford Dictionary*

The shattering of difference like an entrance into fiction. An active bliss of rupture. At the same time my body opens. But a fissure and not the fragment. Opening into the density of matter. One day and the consciousness of a sharp explosion in the slit. Inside the opening all differences are excited since colour is sensation, from mauve to red, difference. Or while the body is being tattooed on the outside. But within my own difference I see clearly.

—Brossard, *These Our Mothers*

Introduction: Women, Reading, Kroetsch

Readers who require the *politesse* of convention should steer clear of this book. They have no business either reading it or railing at it. But if you are a reader willing to free yourself, willing to entertain a literary seduction without manners or morals, then you too will be willing to be entranced as, "coming always to the end, we are free, always, to salvage ourselves. . . . by the lovely treachery of words."

—van Herk review of *The Lovely Treachery of Words*

While Kroetsch is not a feminist writer, he shares many of the concerns of those who are: especially the need to challenge unexamined humanist notions such as centred identity, coherent subjectivity, and aesthetic originality. He offers instead decentred multiplicity, split selves, and double-voiced parody.

—Hutcheon, *The Canadian Postmodern*

Special thanks to Robert Kroetsch who also encouraged this project from the very beginning.

—Neuman and Kamboureli, "Acknowledgements," *A Mazing Space*

That could be seen as a victory for feminism. The Man's order is disturbed by the woman with the impertinent questions and the incisive comments. But as with all seductions, the question of complicity poses itself. The dichotomy active/passive is always equivocal in seduction, that is what distinguishes it from rape.

—Gallop, *The Daughter's Seduction*

We read those field notes, mother and I; together we went through those long and slender notebooks, designed to fit a denim pocket rather than a coffee table. We read in those sun-faded and water-wrinkled books, read not only the words but the squashed mosquitoes, the spiders' legs, the stains of thick black coffee, even the blood that smeared the already barely decipherable words. And the message was always so clear that my mother could read, finally, without unpuzzling the blurred letters or the hasty, intense scrawl. She could read her own boredom and possibly her loneliness, if not his outrageous joy.

—Kroetsch, *Badlands*

Notes to the Introduction can be found on pages 10-11.

If, as E. D. Blodgett argues, Robert Kroetsch "currently dominates, if one person may be said to do so, literary theory in Canadian critical discourse" (12), for the speakers of at least one heterogeneous Canadian critical discourse, Kroetsch's "dominant" theoretical position seems especially problematic. I am speaking, of course, of the speakers of feminist discourses: women. Why, then, should a book deliberately bring together Kroetsch and feminist theory? Is not an appropriation of Kroetsch for feminist purposes a further entrenchment of his dominance?

A prior question poses itself: *do* feminist critics find Kroetsch's (white, male) dominance problematic? Do, or should, only women speak the discourses of feminism? Let me defer discussion of the second issue for a moment and consider first a configuration of women in Kroetsch's most recent collection of selected and new essays, *The Lovely Treachery of Words* (1989), which poses this question for us. Four figures appear in Michael Ondaatje's cover photograph: two women, Kroetsch, and, blurred in the background, what appears to be a jester/trickster. An unsmiling, rather elderly looking, grey-haired, bearded, but living (and life-size), version of Robert Kroetsch is positioned between and behind the two handless, miniaturized statues of unnamed and—to the best of my knowledge—unknown women. Kroetsch's body is cut off at the pelvis; the women's bodies, positioned on either side of him, fill the frame.

Because Kroetsch's head is positioned between them, at waist level, one could argue that in this photograph he occupies the position Blodgett assigns him: the phallic centre. Yet aspects of the photograph undermine this reading; Kroetsch's relation to the women remains ambiguous. His position is simultaneously at the centre, a phallic supplement holding them up—a kind of puppeteer if you like—and yet displaced; he looks at us only through them, from the background. Even further back, the trickster figure looks at all of them and at Kroetsch looking at us. Moreover, the faces of the women express additional ambiguity: one woman looks disdainfully down on Kroestch, the other is happily oblivious to him.

Canadian women critics' reactions to Robert Kroetsch have not been even this clear. While many feminist critics are, for the most part, happily oblivious to his influence,[1] the women who have commented on Kroetsch's work express neither disdain nor disinterest.

To the contrary, the work of women like Shirley Neuman, Linda Hutcheon, and Aritha van Herk, women who often align themselves with feminist issues[2] has helped *produce* what Margaret Turner calls the canonization of Robert Kroetsch. In a recent essay, Turner points out Kroetsch's paradoxical authority within the Canadian intellectual community, what she calls "that *phenomenon* of Kroetsch": "he can count on being heard. . . . His speaking against tradition has served only to place another tradition based on post-structuralism, narratology, intertextuality, and the theories of deconstruction and reader-response criticism" (68). Despite his influence in almost every area of Canadian poststructuralism, however, Turner finds that there has been, finally, no "rigorous feminist analysis" (65) of Kroetsch's texts. The women in the photograph do not, to continue the analogy, speak (or write).

Let me digress for a moment and say that I am particularly interested in the question of feminism and Kroetsch's texts because of my own recent arguments about their (erroneous, I now think) "post-feminism." As Part 1 argues, and as Part 2 illustrates, there is a theory of subjectivity available in Kroetsch's work which is useful for feminism. But I think that the theory of the contradictory subject in Kroetsch—what I would now refer to as the concept of agency—can be located, not so much "in" Kroetsch's texts as in particular *readings* of Kroetsch's texts, readings by women critics like Neuman, Hutcheon, and van Herk. Readings of Kroetsch by women critics have produced the version of Kroetsch's texts—one that finds a decentred, and yet powerful, theory of subjectivity—which feminism may find useful.

Women Read Kroetsch

> The finished book is for that reader I call Ishtar, that undiscoverable and discovered reader towards whom one, always, writes. And, finally, the book, in its incompleteness, is for my two daughters, Meg and Laura, a tenuous suggestion of the ways of a father's love. (Kroetsch, "Author's Note," *Completed Field Notes* 270)

Kroetsch dedicates his "completed" continuing poem, "the finished book," to a woman reader: Ishtar. But Ishtar represents the women readers—"undiscoverable *and* discovered"—"*towards* whom one, always, writes" (italics mine), without expectation of reply. Both whore *and* goddess, her contradictory subjectivity is continually unsettled and unsettling. She is both m(i)s/read and m(i)s/reader.

The "incompleteness" of the continuing poem is for two other women readers: his daughters.

The spectrum of possible women readers created by these dedications is an unusual one. The figure of Ishtar is doubled, contradictory, and inaccessible and yet the "finished" book is for "her"; his daughters, presumably present and able to read the book, are called upon to continually "refinish" the incompleteness of the book.

Women critics reading Kroetsch take various places along this range of possible positions. Sometimes rereading daughters, sometimes momentarily seduced Ishtars, there is no single response to Kroetsch among women readers.

The Woman Reader in the Text

Shirley Neuman's collegial and supportive relationship with Kroetsch and Kroetsch's texts began with the publication of *Labyrinths of Voice* in 1982. A three-way conversation between Neuman, Kroetsch, and Robert Wilson, the text is constructed as a labyrinth of voices which, in its inclusion of citations (scattered throughout the conversation, variously supporting and undermining the speakers' positions) from contemporary theoretical texts and its departure from the traditional interview form, is very much a multi-authored (even unauthorized) text literally produced by readings of the speakers' words, their words in relation to the citations, and our readings of these multiple juxtapositions.

Neuman's 1984 essay, "Figuring the Reader, Figuring the Self in *Field Notes*," although not overtly feminist in orientation, also makes a compelling point about reading, and the reader, in Kroetsch's poetry which is useful to my argument. The reader constructed by the text of *Field Notes*, Neuman argues, is a woman. Moreover, Neuman locates in *Field Notes* what is arguably already a feminist rhetorical strategy in Kroetsch's novel *Badlands*: the narrator, Anna, tells a (tall) tale based on her reading of her father's field notes. In Neuman's reading of Kroetsch, she takes up and parodies the "daughter's" position: Kroetsch's *Field Notes* (like Dawe's) are available to us only through Neuman's (like Anna's) reading.

By locating the reader in Kroetsch's continuing poem as female, Neuman can argue that it is only "in response to his daughter's questions" (in "Delphi: Commentary") that the poet is "able to give words to the voice" (189). The book, in its incompleteness, is for his daughters. The poem is a product of his daughter's questions. Women readers, like the daughters in "Delphi: Commentary," construct the poem: "Delphi, as Kroetsch figures it, is its commentaries, the intersection of all the past and all the future readings of the site" (186). Neuman's point, too, is that what we usually speak of as "Kroetsch's" continuing poem is, self-consciously, its readings. My version of Kroetsch's texts—the one I find useful for feminism—is, self-consciously, its readings by women. Neuman makes much of the "new word"—autobiographillyria—which she sees as the textual inscription of the female reader. For Neuman, autobiographillyria is a genre which offers the possibility of a simultaneously constructed and constructive version of self; it is a "genre in which the self is unstable, undermined, subject to doublings, displacements, transformations" (192). Neuman's reading of this new genre also allows later women readers of Kroetsch to find, in Kroetsch's texts, a theory of the feminist subject.

Postmodern Feminism

With the recent publication of, not only *The Canadian Postmodern* (1988), but also *A Poetics of Postmodernism* (1988), and *The Politics of Postmodernism* (1989), Linda Hutcheon has gained a very visible authority within the community of Canadian readers and writers. In Hutcheon's repeated attempts to negotiate the agendas of feminism and postmodernism we find, as the quote from Hutcheon which I used as one of the epigraphs to this chapter suggests, an attempt to align Kroetsch with feminist issues. In *A Poetics of Postmodernism* she says, however,

> although feminism has had a major impact on the direction and focus of postmodernism, I would not want to equate the feminist with the postmodern for two reasons. First, this would obscure the many different kinds of feminisms that exist. . . . But even more important, to co-opt the feminist project into the unresolved and contradictory postmodern one would be to simplify and undo the important political agenda of feminism. (xi-xii)

Hutcheon's own position is currently, as she says in *The Canadian Postmodern*, "some mix of feminism and (what was labelled) poststructuralism" (vii). And yet Hutcheon seems to be unaware of her own act of reading, her own deliberate construction of a version of Kroetsch's texts which is useful to feminism. Consider again the following:

> While Kroetsch is not a feminist writer, he shares many of the concerns of those who are: especially the need to challenge unexamined humanist notions such as centred identity, coherent subjectivity, and aesthetic originality. He offers instead decentred multiplicity, split selves, and double-voiced parody. (*The Canadian Postmodern* 161-72)

Who is the "he," the Kroetsch who "is not a feminist writer"? Where and how does "he share" *his* concerns? In what way is *he* "offering"? It would be more accurate to say that *Hutcheon* locates in these texts challenges to liberal humanism, decentredness, double-voiced parody, etc. The textual strategies employed in novels like *Badlands*, *Alibi*, and *The Studhorse Man*, or in the *Completed Field Notes*, do not include the kind of obviousness implied in a word like "offering." Kroetsch does not offer us anything. We produce the texts ourselves.

"Our Hero of Language"

Aritha van Herk, an Alberta writer-critic like Kroetsch, has engaged rhetorically with Kroetsch's texts in a number of ways, including her own feminist rewriting of *The Studhorse Man* in *No Fixed Address*.[3] In the "Biocritical Essay" which prefaces the University of Calgary's inventory of its archival collection of Kroetsch's papers, van Herk calls Kroetsch "our hero of language" (xxxv). In her ficto-critical (dis)missive, "no parrot/no crow/no parrot," she writes, "Dear Kroetsch, Swore I'd never write another line about you" (12). But she has written other lines. Specifically, her most recent writing on Kroetsch is a rather more scholarly review of *The Lovely Treachery of Words*, which appeared in *The Globe and Mail* in 1989. The language with which van Herk describes Kroetsch's reception by hostile (most often male) readers suggests what for her continues to be the potential power in Kroetsch's textual strategies. She says that Kroetsch often "offends" and is perceived to be "dangerous" in his criticism; that a reader will feel either hostility or excitement when confronted with his work; but that the "adventurous reader" will be "utterly seduced" by Kroetsch.

Her review pays special attention to the last essay in the collection. In Kroetsch's "My Book is Bigger than Yours," a reading of *A Mazing Space: Writing Canadian Women Writing*, van Herk finds an argument for a "feminist dialectic." She applauds Kroetsch's self-consciousness about his vulnerability before feminist writing, which, in her words (and that these are *her* words is significant), Kroetsch sees as "occupying the cutting edge, as having cracked open the boundaries of language and thought" (van Herk 3). Again, a woman critic deliberately defends the work of Kroetsch and appropriates his work on language for feminist purposes.

Disparate as they remain, readings of Kroetsch's texts produced by women tend to foreground a relation between subjectivity and language which is potentially useful to feminism. It is at this juncture that I, too, find Kroetsch's work most valuable. The question remains, what kind of feminist work is it (and is it feminist work) to foreground texts written by a man in light of poststructuralist theories of language and subjectivity?

Feminism and the Metaphor of the "Post"

> In the absence of a stable meaning, the questions one addresses to a text or linguistic marker become, in Foucault's words, by whom, for whom, in whose interest: the interests being served by the term postfeminism seem to me to be those opposed to the ideological frame with which you inscribe the term. . . . After all, there has never been any talk of postpatriarchy, so how can there be a post-feminism? There hasn't even been feminism yet. (Godard letter of 30 November 1987)

> The need for feminist theory to continue its radical critique of dominant discourses on gender, such as these are, even as they attempt to do away with sexual difference altogether, is all the more pressing since the word *postfeminism* has been spoken, and not in vain. This kind of deconstruction of the subject is effectively a way to recontain women in femininity (Woman) and to reposition female subjectivity *in* the male subject, however that will be defined. (de Lauretis, *Technologies of Gender* 24)

An earlier version of my argument spoke of a "post-feminist" theory which could accommodate the implications of the split subject for our understanding of sexual identity.[4] Drawing on Derrida's use of the metaphor of the "post" in *The Post Card*, I argued that "post-feminism" may be "after" and "behind" feminism in that it describes feminism in a *post*-postal era: "the one in the other, the one in front of the other, the one after the other, the one behind the other" (*The Post Card* 19). I now think that this attitude in feminist thinking might better be labelled deconstructive feminism, or, as a colleague of mine aptly suggested, the feminization of deconstruction,[5] with all of the contradictory resonances that such an uneasy alliance generates. Feminism's appropriation of deconstruction empowers women readers to recognize that all male cultural paradigms, including deconstruction, are constituted within ideological practices which are themselves contradictory and so have the potential to betray their own agendas, to tell the differences within.[6] But what I did not consider at the time were the vast number of women readers for whom the primary connotations of the word "postfeminist" would not be these. I agree with de Lauretis, who suggests that the appearance of postfeminism is evidence that feminist theory must continue its research into the "technologies of gender."

Consider, for example, the May 1988 issue of *Cosmopolitan*, in which Marilyn Stasio uses the term "postfeminism" to describe a lack of political energy among young women. Clearly, "postfeminism" in this context is a feminism which has lost its revolutionary force and so is not feminism at all. In "The Feminist Movement: Where We Stand Today," Stasio writes,

> The movement is in trouble. . . . Despite recent victories in the courts—including two landmark decisions favoring women on key issues of maternity leave and affirmative action hiring practices—outsiders view the movement's so-called postfeminist phase as drained of energy, its members disoriented on the issues and deeply divided over the future. (262)

"The question, ultimately," says Stasio, "is how each one of us defines herself as a woman. Equal to men—only special? Or equal to men—only different? Or equal to men—only special and different in ways that don't substantially matter?" (264). A recent editorial reply to Erica Jong in *The New York Times Book Review* by novelist Nora

Johnson situates another place of difficulty for feminist thinkers. Johnson justified what Jong described as her problematic methodology by suggesting it offered "possible new directions for the intellectually exhausted concept of feminism" (49).

The perceived decline of feminism's radical potential has not remained outside the academy. As early as 1981 Alice Jardine produced an alternative feminist critical practice which she called "gynesis" for a Modern Language Association special session: "New Directions in Feminist Critical Theories in France and the Francophone World." Jardine's effort was also a self-conscious attempt to salvage feminism for intellectuals, especially for thinkers working out of the French intellectual tradition. But is a feminist theory which works with French theories of language necessarily a *post*feminism?

The difficulty here is that I am attempting to bring together the political agenda of liberal feminism with the intellectual context of French poststructuralist theory. As Janet Todd summarizes, those we refer to as the French "feminists," Kristeva, Cixous, Irigaray, were "united in disapproving of intellectual modes claiming to reveal an empirical reality or an unproblematized history, and they were dubious of any efforts at scrutinizing the surface manifestations of women's oppression; instead the usually hidden body, the unconscious, the deep structures of culture and language, were their data" (50). Less empirical and more idealist, the philosophical tradition out of which the "new French feminists" work is one which accommodates the interrogation of language and subjectivity which I described as postfeminist because it *is* a different kind of feminism, one which sees the possibility of change as occurring on a different plane. Because it arises out of two philosophically different sets of assumptions about how to effect change, I experience my own feminist critical practice as continually contradictory, an uneasy mix of Western liberal feminism and French poststructuralism; I speak here, then, from the place of dislocation that I seek to describe. I did not write this at a single point in time or with a single "vision." Considering how readers are, like the texts we read, shaped by the discourses of our culture *and* how we are able to speak and effect change—how we are both subjects and agents—is necessary to account for the changes that feminism has brought about, including the changes in my own thinking that have arisen as a result of the research for this book.

In Chapters One and Two, I discuss, respectively, the potentially feminist theory of subjectivity I locate in Kroetsch's texts and the implications for the female subject of poststructuralist theory which Kroetsch has been instrumental in introducing into the Canadian intellectual community. In Chapters Three through Eight, I read a number of Kroetsch's texts to interrogate further the possibility of constructing a feminist theory of subjectivity out of the writing of a biological male. In the final chapter I consider the implications of this theory of subjectivity for future feminist and other work.

Notes

1 For example, the work of the feminist collective *Tessera*—Barbara Godard, Daphne Marlatt, Gail Scott, Kathy Mezei—which Blodgett describes as producing the most significant changes in Canadian criticism at present—has been concerned primarily with, as the collective says in its subscription information, publishing "the theoretical and experimental writing of Québécoise and English-Canadian feminist writers." Only Barbara Godard has written specifically on Kroetsch. See her "Other Fictions: Robert Kroetsch's Criticism."

2 See Neuman and Kamboureli's *A Mazing Space: Writing Canadian Women Writing*; Hutcheon's preface to *The Canadian Postmodern* in which she describes her current position as some mix of feminism and poststructuralism; van Herk's recent novels and "ficto-criticism" which make overtly feminist gestures in their challenges to patriarchal literary-critical convention.

3 I am grateful to Barbara Godard for her suggestion that van Herk's novels are often a rewriting of Kroetsch "in the feminine." Linda Hutcheon makes a similar argument in a review of *No Fixed Address* in which she considers the novel a "female and feminist version of the travelling salesman" and suggests that in the background of van Herk's novel is Kroetsch's essay "The Fear of Women in Prairie Fiction: An Erotics of Space": "In *No Fixed Address*, van Herk offers an alternative to Kroetsch's comic resolution of horse/house (into whore's house) in her image of the 1959 black Mercedes driven by her heroine—who lives IN it and also moves along the road of the west ON its wheels. . . . But van Herk's protagonist manages to use travel not to evade but to enable—even provoke—the sexual" (107); indeed, Arachne "travels to travel. Her only paradox is arriving somewhere, her only solution is to leave for somewhere else" (*No Fixed Address* 164). My suggestion that van Herk's novel is a rewriting, in the feminine, of *The Studhorse Man* needs elaboration for there is a sense in which *The Studhorse Man* is itself a rewriting, in the feminine, of travel literature and of the traditional Western, a sense in which Kroetsch and van Herk are participating in the same feminizing of form. Kroetsch's "novel," the biography of Hazard Lepage, is also what van Herk's "missing" narrator repeatedly subtitles her book: a (or rather several) "Notebook[s] on a missing person." But van Herk's feminizing is both playfully covert and overt: the travelling salesman

is a woman—Arachne Manteia—who sells "underthings"; her "confidante" is a feminist: "Only Thena gets the whole truth. For what is a traveler without a confidante? It is impossible to fictionalize a life without someone to oversee the journey. And Thena is the perfect confidante, discreet if opinionated. She is trustworthy, reliable. She has always watched with a clear eye and a bitter disregard for tender feelings, even her own" (154). Thena is not, however, the narrator. Arachne's story is unfinished, ambiguous. She remains a missing person. Constructed out of multiple stories, we cannot address her with any certainty because, of course, she has no fixed address.

4 I now both regret and reject the label "post-feminist" which I used in "How *The Studhorse Man* Makes Love: A Postfeminist Analysis" and throughout my doctoral dissertation. Regardless of my desire to appropriate the term for feminist purposes, it continues to signify a phase "after" feminism. In my current work, I prefer to see the project of undermining binary oppositions as necessarily a feminist project.

5 I am grateful to Ashraf Rushdy for his useful phrase.

6 The question of feminism's relation to deconstruction is a highly complex one. There is no question that the man who is seen as the originator of the deconstructive method, Jacques Derrida, has had a highly problematic relationship with women, women's texts, and women critics. Lola Lemire Tostevin presents the problem succinctly in *'sophie*, her feminist rewriting of philosophy: "In spite of the claims that his deconstructive method of analysis allies itself with the voiceless, the marginal and the repressed, Jacques Derrida doesn't much care for questions by women. During the seminars of his two week course, The Political Theology of Language, he spends at least fifteen minutes disseminating most questions from men, while he only spends two or three minutes disseminating questions from women and even then he manages to trivialize them to the point of eliciting laughs from the class. If in his texts, Derrida likes to question the master, in his classes master and students stay in their respective places. In Derrida's seminars women remain seminally divided. Keep to the margins to bear witness to what he tells" (45: I am grateful to Frank Davey for drawing this passage to my attention). Nonetheless, feminist theory and criticism in Canada and elsewhere have continued to support, question, challenge, and reconfigure deconstruction. Cf., for example, essays by Neuman, Hutcheon, van Herk, Kamboureli, Hlus, Harasym, Théoret, Tostevin, Freiwald, Williamson, in *A Mazing Space: Writing Canadian Women Writing*. Only if we insist on the final authority of Derrida in/over the methods of deconstruction do we draw the problematic relation between Derrida and women into every occasion of deconstructive practice.

PART ONE

Reading Woman

CHAPTER ONE

Telling as Difference: Feminism, Subjectivity, Kroetsch

> I AM/naught. That's all I is. Mmmmmmmmmmm.
> —Kroetsch, "After Paradise," *Completed Field Notes*

> It is precisely in that space of contradiction, in the double and self-subverting coherence of its narrative grammar and figural ambiguities, that the film addresses me, spectator, *as a(-)woman.*
> —de Lauretis, "Strategies of Coherence," *Technologies of Gender*

This book considers whether a feminist theory of subjectivity can be constructed out of the writing of Canadian postmodernist poet-critic-novelist-theorist Robert Kroetsch. I begin with the words "I AM/naught," from the outrageous completion of his continuing poem *Field Notes*, because they offer an exemplary articulation of this theory of subjectivity in Kroetsch's texts. By speaking "I AM" and "naught" speaking, the shifter "I" is both affirmed and undermined, given a place of meaningful inscription and caught up in the meanings of its inscription. The "Mmmmmmmmmmm" following "That's all I is" signifies a delight in the possibility that identity is a "nothing" issue. But the repetition of the "I" and the capitalized "I AM" simultaneously affirm identity even as the speaker's "presence" is made self-consciously textual by the grammar of the "That's all I is."

Critical analysis of subjectivity—feminist and otherwise—stands at the same difficult crossroads. Both the positioning and the agency of the subject (the psychoanalytic, neo-Marxist term for the self) are vital areas of inquiry in both literary and social theory. For example, Paul Smith, in *Discerning the Subject*, seeks a notion of subjectivity

The note to Chapter One is found on page 26.

which will "satisfy both the demands of theory and the exigencies of practice" (xxxii). Considered variously as the "*actor* who follows ideological scripts" or the "*agent* who reads them in order to insert him/herself into them—or not," Smith locates, in feminism, the "I" that I—and the women critics writing on Kroetsch who informed this reading of Kroetsch—find in Kroetsch's work: an actor who is her (or his) own agent, a necessary "double-play" which breaks down "the old habit of *presuming* the 'subject' as the fixed guarantor of a given epistemological formation" and casts doubt on "the adequacy of the poststructuralist shibboleth of the decentred 'subject'" (151). The contradictions which arise are, Smith argues, "perhaps capable of providing some important cues for the question of how an active political agent can be dis-cerned from the sub-jected subject" (xxxiv-xxxv, 135).

As I mentioned in the introduction, an earlier version of my argument, published in *Canadian Literature*, took a quite different approach. I argued then that if the gendering of the subject (becoming a woman or a man) occurs at the level of subjection rather than agency, a fairly simple deconstruction of the subject dissolves the difference between the sexes and makes the use of a male writer for feminist purposes legitimate; "the" difference between male and female is dissolved. If the subject is not the centre of meaning and consciousness, I argued, telling the difference between the two sexes becomes a telling of differences within the one decentred subject, a figure abundantly available in Kroetsch's work, from the doubly doubled William William Dorfendorf in *Alibi* to the Robert Kroetsch of *Robert Kroetsch: Essays*.

Seductive as this argument may have been "in theory," as we say, in practice (something "I/I," as junior, untenured, female member of an English department am entirely dislocated within), "the" subject, as it is conceived of "in theory," is never gender specific. As sophisticated a theorist as Teresa de Lauretis can speak of the Althusserian subject of ideology and the Lacanian misrecognized subject as "ungendered" even as she recognizes that "neither of these systems considers the possibility—let alone the process of constitution—of a female subject" (*Technologies of Gender* 6). But the subject which is not female is not gender neutral either. With Robert Scholes, my feeling now "is that until no one notices or cares about the difference we had better not pretend it isn't there" ("Reading Like a Man" 217). Locating how those differences are "there," in Kroetsch's texts, is one of the subjects of this inquiry.

Consider the assumed meaning of the word "woman" in this excerpt from Kroetsch's essay "Beyond Nationalism": "In the beginning is the artist, beginning. With the difference that in Canadian writing the artist-figure is often a woman" (85). By the word "woman" Kroetsch *tells* us he means "women" like Mrs. Bentley, the narrator of Sinclair Ross's *As For Me and My House*; or "Audrey Thomas' self-surrogate in *Latakia*"; or the "nameless female narrator in Margaret Atwood's *Surfacing*" (85). But by saying that "the difference" in Canadian writing is that the artist figure is a woman, Kroetsch's *words* tell us also—this difference is one I am telling—that otherwise, without saying that the artist-figure is often a woman—the artist figure is assumed to be a man. The word "artist" signifies a male person.

Being able to tell certain kinds of differences—between women and men, between women's and men' writings—has been a major concern in much feminist literary theory. But knowing who is writing is a knowledge based on the certainty of difference. The argument generally goes in one of two ways. Elaine Showalter, Sandra Gilbert, and Susan Gubar argue—with the uneasy support of liberal political philosophy—that if there are differences they should not make a difference. Women, and women's writing, should have equal access to power in the social or literary order. In seeming contrast, feminists working out of such vastly different philosophical and political contexts as Luce Irigaray and Adrienne Rich argue that there *are* differences, and they should make a difference. While Hélène Cixous—in "The Laugh of the Medusa"—allows that some men, like Genet or Kleist, have produced *écriture féminine*, women like Irigaray and Rich celebrate "women's writing" as a site of particularly feminine *jouissance* that cannot be produced by biological men. Each argument assumes there is a difference *between* the binary opposites man/woman.

In *The Critical Difference*, Barbara Johnson describes a rather different reading strategy in which "the differences 'between' entities (prose and poetry, man and woman, literature and theory, guilt and innocence) are shown to be based on a repression of differences *within* entities, ways in which an entity differs from itself" (x). As de Lauretis points out in *Technologies of Gender*, there are significant differences within the concept of "woman." For example, women are constructed as both viewers (in literary terms, women are readers) and as the "viewed" figure on the screen (or in the text).

The following sentence can be read to suggest the theory of difference I am describing, one which sees all telling as a telling of difference: "a word is an intersection where things can happen; writers are forever misreading words" (Kroetsch, *Labyrinths of Voice* 149). For example, I can misread the word "woman" in Kroetsch's earlier statement from "Beyond Nationalism" to suggest that if, in the beginning of writing in Canada, "the artist-figure is often a woman," "she" is also one of those "real" women writers whose writing "began" the tradition we speak of as Canadian: Anna Jameson, Susanna Moodie, Isabella Valancy Crawford. The word "woman" always signifies both women as historical subjects and woman as literary or other representation. To discourage these multiple meanings of the word is to "repress the difference." "Woman" is both and always at least doubly significative: here—present as an agent for change in the world—and elsewhere—re-presented in a text. The question is not, how can I tell the difference, but how can I tell anything but differences. In a quite useful and hopeful sense, "difference is articulation" (Derrida, *Of Grammatology* 66).

The difference within woman—between *woman* and *women* in the sense articulated by de Lauretis—is homologous to Benveniste's linguistic difference within the subject—between the "I" of the enunciation and the "I" of the enounced. When I say "I am a woman" the "I" that *I* speak with is split between two, often elided, positions. "I" am subject both of the signifier—"I say, 'I am a woman'"—and to the signified—"I am a woman." Sentences such as "I am not lying when I say I am a woman" tell the differences within the speaking subject.

The post-Freudian psychoanalytic theory of identity which I take up in the next chapter is also a theory of difference. Since Freud, the conscious intention of the subject in the act of speaking has been radically called into question. But Jacques Lacan's rereading of Freud, particularly his theory of the mirror stage in the constitution of the self, depends on an understanding of identity very like Benveniste's formulation. Like Benveniste, Lacan's speaking subject is "othered."

The small child, in taking an identity, sees its self in a mirror, as an other, as a separate character that exists "over there." In a now notorious linguistic and philosophical assault on the Cartesian ego Lacan enacts this displacement of the identifying subject: "I think where I am not, therefore I am where I do not think" ("The Agency of the Letter" 166): "I" inhabit a series of what may be called ex/positions, former positions, positions desired but never held (at least not exclusively).

Homologous to de Lauretis's difference within woman, is neo-Marxist philosopher Louis Althusser's famous difference between the concrete individual and the subject. In his essay on the function of ideology in society, Althusser notes that although there is initially a difference between the two, to enter a social formation we must be "interpellated," or called upon, by the seemingly singular and replete subject positions available to us. Words from a poem by the Maritime writer Robert Gibbs describe the workings of ideology: in effect, ideology says,

> Hey you there insisting you are
> there
> Hey I have you here.
> (*All This Night Long* 8)

In order to speak we take up these positions in the social world that efface alternatives, contradictions, and differences. The "over there" becomes, finally, our "here."

The subject remains a subject in difference, however, both subject in a world and subject to a world. The differences within the meanings of the word "subject" appear in quite ordinary usage:

> In the ordinary use of the term, subject in fact means: (1) a free subjectivity, a centre of initiatives, author of and responsible for its actions [de Lauretis's women as readers]; (2) a subjected being, who submits to a higher authority, and is therefore stripped of all freedom except that of freely accepting *his* submission [italics added; note Althusser's use of the pronoun "his"—apparently not only women but men, too, are "subject" to the representations offered by the ideologies within which we are inscribed]. (Althusser 182)

"The" difference is not *only between* two stable entities but *within* what the deconstructionists call already decentred subjects. I am a woman reading, yes, but I know myself as a woman through the representations of woman that I have necessarily appropriated. And, as Althusser points out, not only woman but man is constituted as a subject subjected to representations.

If both man and woman are subject and subjected, self and other, how do we talk about the relation supposedly "between" them? Derrida would look to the differences within the subject as having an important bearing on the relation between subjects and articulates this complexity of differential relations—tells the difference—with that now infamous word which, in French, sounds the same as difference, but is spelled with an "a" instead of an "e" in the last syllable. *Différance* plays on and between the meanings of both differ and defer. For Derrida, the play of meaning which arises out of such spelling mistakes are "gifts" which disrupt our commonsense assumptions about meaning, interrupt what he identifies as our belief in the postal structure which assumes that things sent (including words and letters) are always received intact. These "gifts" offer the possibility of ideological change:

> when we speak of sexual difference we must distinguish between opposition and difference. Opposition is two, opposition is man/woman. Difference on the other hand, can be an indefinite number of sexes and once there is sexual difference in its classical sense—an opposition of two—the arrangement is such that the gift is impossible. All that you can call "gift"—love, *jouissance*—is absolutely forbidden, is forbidden by the dual opposition. ("Women in the Beehive" 198)

Stephen Heath agrees when he writes, in an article on "Male Feminism," "There is no sexual *relation* because there are never two *sexes* but one and the other on both sides of the 'relation'. . . . One is always in my or yourself one and the other" (21). Patriarchal authority and logocentrism depend on the maintenance of difference as opposition. So, too, necessarily and problematically enough, has much feminist practice.

Feminist anthropologist Sherry Ortner's "Is Female to Male as Nature Is to Culture?" takes for granted both the "universality of female subordination" and the binary oppositions female/male and nature/culture, as if each side of the oppositions did not necessarily have its part in the other. It would be more accurate to say, with

Dorothy Dinnerstein, that human beings are "naturally unnatural." We are naturally cultural. Dinnerstein gives as an example of the cultural construction of our natures that we do not walk "naturally" upright:

> such ills as fallen arches, lower back pain, and hernias testify that the body has not adapted itself completely to the upright posture. Yet this unnatural position, forced on the unwilling body by the project of tool-using, is precisely what has made possible the development of important aspects of our "nature": the hand and the brain, and the complex system of skills, language, and social arrangements which were both effects and causes of hand and brain. . . . We are what we have made ourselves, and we must continue to make ourselves as long as we exist at all. (*The Mermaid and the Minotaur* 21-22)

"We are," says Dinnerstein, "what we have made ourselves, and we must continue to make ourselves as long as we exist at all" (22). The essentialist assumptions within literary feminism are not so easy to dispel. Elaine Showalter's very influential essay "Feminist Criticism in the Wilderness," makes a pioneering distinction between two forms of feminist criticism, what Showalter calls feminist critique and gynocritics. For Showalter, "feminist critique" or "feminist reading" is "a mode of interpretation" which "reasserts the authority of experience" (182; 181). For Showalter, feminist reading is based on the authority of the extra-textual female. Her "woman reader" is not, as Jonathan Culler tries to argue in *On Deconstruction*, a woman reading "as a woman" (64). By "woman reader" Showalter means biological women reading texts as feminists because they "consider the images and stereotypes of women in literature, the omissions and misconceptions about women in criticism, and woman-as-sign in semiotic systems" (182). Problematically, this feminist literary practice generally finds only patriarchal representations of women in texts written by biological men. It does not acknowledge useful, or even contradictory, representations of women in male-authored texts, or problematic representations of women in female-authored texts. It is a criticism centred, after all, on the author. Feminist critique, because of its methodology, cannot locate moments in which stable sexual subject positions are undermined and so reinforces the binary difference between male-authored and female-authored writing.

Gynocriticism, concerned as it is, not with a(-)woman, but with *the* woman as writer, does not seek to undermine sexual subject positions, does not show the ways that we speak from places that are constituted by contradictory differences within. Not that the vacillation between sexual subject positions only occurs in the writing of biological men. In Virginia Woolf's *Orlando*, for example, Orlando (as a man) wakes one morning to discover that, contrary to all grammatical sense, "he was a woman" (86). Although Orlando is both [and neither] a man and/or a woman, he and/or she, "in future we must, for convention's sake," says the fictional biographer, "say 'her' for 'his' and 'she' for 'he'" (87).

Consider further the vacillation between and within sexual subject positions in the following passage from *Orlando*:

> She was horrified to perceive how low an opinion she was forming of the other sex, the manly, to which it had once been her pride to belong. "To fall from a mast-head," she thought "because you see a woman's ankles; to dress up like a Guy Fawkes and parade the streets, so that women may praise you; to deny a woman teaching lest she may laugh at you; to be the slave of the frailest chit in petticoats, and yet to go about as if you were the Lords of creation.—Heavens!" she thought, "what fools they make of us—what fools we are!" *And here it would seem from some ambiguity in her terms that she was censuring both sexes equally, as if she belonged to neither; and indeed, for the time being, she seemed to vacillate; she was man; she was woman.* (99; italics added)

This passage illustrates what Julia Kristeva calls the "third attitude" in feminist thinking in which "the very dichotomy man/woman as an opposition between two rival entities may be understood as belonging to *metaphysics*. What can 'identity,' even 'sexual identity,' mean in a new theoretical and scientific space where the very notion of identity is challenged?" ("Women's Time" 32).

My reading of Kroetsch's writing belongs to this third attitude in feminist thinking. While it is certainly true that Kroetsch's texts are male-authored, if the questions we ask of them are not only who wrote them but what they are doing when a woman reads them we can locate the ways their incessant challenges to notions of self, origin, truth, and meaning are allied with feminist practice. When read by a woman with a specific feminist purpose in mind, Kroetsch's texts can usefully show us how "the" difference between male-authored and female-authored writing—indeed between binary oppositions of all kinds—is undermined.

In an often-cited conversation with Margaret Laurence in *Creation* Kroetsch says, "In a sense, we haven't got an identity until somebody tells our story. The fiction makes us real" (63). The fiction of sexual identity also makes us real men and women. But how we know ourselves to be sexual subjects is not inevitable, or natural, or simple. In "Realism in Art," the Russian formalist Roman Jakobson notes that we must know the conventions to see the real; only then does what we call "recognition" become "spontaneous." If we "recognize" ourselves as men or women only by appropriating the conventions of sexual identity, through the fictions available to us, we are sexually identified (and identifiable) by *playing* at being men and women. Kroetsch writes in "For Play and Entrance": "As we come to the end of self, in our century, we come again to the long poem. We become again, persons in the world, against the preposterous notion of self. We are each our own crossroads" (107). The self as a crossroads, constituted in and at play, is a liberating one for our understanding of both identity and sexual difference. If "we are each our own crossroads" and we "play" at being men and women, our sexuality is traversed by both one and the other.

Robert Kroetsch's work challenges sexual difference by seeing it as textual difference, points out the ways our readings of ourselves, including our sexual selves, are always misreadings, tellings of differences. In *Labyrinths of Voice* Kroetsch says,

> You can take ten *tellings* of the Oedipus story, say, and observe that they are all alike, but you can also take ten tellings and observe how they are all different from each other. I think that what we are doing now is moving to that second class of question: how are tellings different from each other? (131)

If we are moving to that second class of question, how do we tell the differences inherent in the appropriation of sexual identity? What is it to tell?

Even my attempt to tell what telling is is a telling of differences. I can never stop the play of meaning in a text which, as I write, writes me. *The Oxford English Dictionary* definitions of the word "tell" confirm that telling is an ambiguous activity. I read the primary definition—"to give a detailed account of"—to suggest two quite contrary activities—those of writing and speech. Telling is *giving* a detailed account of. This reading of the meaning of the word assumes that a speaker is there, giving the account. But telling is also giving a detailed *account* of. In this reading of the word, I emphasize that even when we speak we are giving an "account," a narrative, a story that is dependent on a written version of the words we are speaking and so is endlessly open to misinterpretation. As writer of these words I am also a continual (mis)reader. I cannot help but tell the differences.

Telling is both giving information about (which assumes telling is an unproblematic activity and truth is accessible) and *trying* to determine (an extremely problematic, if not impossible, activity which the "literal" meaning of the cliché "you never can tell" betrays). The multiple meanings of the word "tell" tell us that whenever we desire to tell the truth—about our experiences about our *selves*—our words tell on us, betray us, "reveal a secret" and "inform against us." You never *can* tell what the truth is, what the fiction is; you never can *tell* the w/hole truth anyway. Telling is difference.

The play of meaning in the word "telling" problematizes the seeming (and *seaming*) opposition between fiction and reality, between giving advice to our friends and publishing a book called *Advice to My Friends*. What we call our "real" world depends on our not acknowledging, certainly not problematizing, the contradiction; it sees *the* world in terms of homologous either/or categories. In a very provocative argument, Ashraf Jamal writes that Kroetsch "attempts to replace an either/or logic with one which says both and. . . . Such a writing necessarily works against systems, at once sutures and ruptures meaning. It is a writing which must ceaselessly place itself under erasure" (17). Robert Kroetsch's texts celebrate the ambiguity and contradiction of a world of both and. . . .

Feminist theory continues to articulate a theory of difference because "difference" has been appropriated by all sides in the feminist debate, both celebrated and implicated in the work of patriarchy. The argument that women's difference should not exclude us from positions of power stands in useful, because unsettling, opposition to the argument that difference is the *source* of our empowerment.

However, in both cases the either/or logic is maintained. I am suggesting that a theory of difference which begins in and with the contradictions takes place in that space of feminist inquiry which sees difference not as natural or stable or unchanging but as social and textual and always in excess of itself.

Kroetsch addresses the tension between the desire to tell and the impossibility of telling when he writes, "there is, in much Canadian writing, a tension between, on the one hand, the desperate need to count, to list, to catalogue . . . and, on the other, the terrible modern suspicion that the counting is being done in a slightly mad dream" ("The Canadian Writer" 14). Kroetsch's long poem, *Seed Catalogue*, articulates this tension, tells this difference, in its title. It "catalogues"—counts, lists, contains, tells—the "seed"—word, play, beginning, absence—that is endlessly dispersing and (re)producing. In words we have no direct access to things; words refer "uncircumventably" to other words (like seed catalogues, lists, ledgers), other writings. The word "telling" itself invokes the contradictions within, which suggest a feminist reader can find the "post-man" Kroetsch no longer able to deliver *the* male. For Kroetsch, the writer writes "as a(-)woman"—Demeter, Anna, Peter, Johnnie, William William—Scheherezades all, who must, in Kroetsch's words, "go on telling stories," telling differences: "She, the teller, as the telling goes on, becomes the tale. . . . As we too. . . . As we too. . . ." ("Contemporary Standards in the Canadian Novel" 45).

I began with one of Kroetsch's readings of "woman": "In the beginning is the artist, beginning. With the difference that in Canadian writing the artist-figure is often a woman." I end with one of Kroetsch's readings of "man":

> The male, certainly, to make his radical beginning, takes on the role of orphan or cowboy or outlaw. He approaches [I misread this to mean "comes nearer to being," "becomes like"] the female. He approaches the garden. He approaches the house. . . .
>
> And only then does he realize he has defined himself out of all entering. ("The Fear of Women in Prairie Fiction" 55)

"To make his radical beginning," to write, "he" becomes fatherless, out(side the)law; "he" refuses "his" position. The "teller" becomes the tale; as we write we are written; we are, to paraphrase the title of one of Kroetsch's novels, "exiles" from our tellings; we are "writings." To "be" in (a-)writing is to recognize the impossibilities of self-presence, of origin, of truth. To write and to recognize that we are always already written is to "be" male only by assuming an alibi.[1] To write is to approach the woman.

Note

1 As Ashraf Jamal notes in his reading of Kroetsch, "alibi" signifies both "elsewhere" and a "*plea* that when an alleged act took place one was elsewhere" (Jamal 5): In speaking, "I" am both here (in my plea) and elsewhere.

CHAPTER TWO

Reading A(-)Woman: Psychoanalysis, Subjectivity, Sexuality

> I am my own emptiness, trying to fill my emptiness with words.
>
> —Kroetsch, *Advice to My Friends*

The word "a(-)woman" in the title of this chapter generates an ambiguous semantic space like the reading I construct here: a self-conscious feminist rereading of Freud which is simultaneously a reading of the concept of "woman" as it is inscribed in the texts of psychoanalysis. I invoke this double inscription as another example of what Smith calls feminism's "double play," to underline my contradictory position as both woman read (subject) and woman reader (agent). Here, in detail, is what feminist film theorist Teresa de Lauretis speaks of as the difference between woman as historical subject (woman reading), and woman as a product of representations (woman read):

> Represented as the negative term of sexual differentiation, spectacle-fetish or specular image, in any case ob-scene, woman is constituted as the ground of representation, the looking-glass held up to man. But, as historical individual, the female viewer is also positioned in the films of classical cinema as spectator-subject; she is thus doubly bound to that very representation which calls on her directly, engages her desire, elicits her pleasure, frames her identification, and makes her complicit in the production of (her) woman-ness. (*Alice Doesn't* 15)

In this chapter I consider the "place" of the metaphor of woman in psychoanalytic theory, with preliminary gestures towards Kroetsch's writing. Following Freud, I ask not what a woman is, but how the concept of "woman," traditionally defined as absence, lack, other, madness (Kroetsch's "emptiness") figures (as) the decentred subject ("I am my own emptiness") in language at the same time as "she" is ("I" am) capable of reading that configuration. What is it to take up the doubled position implied in de Lauretis's term, "a(-)woman"?

In *Reading Woman,* a feminist analysis of the function of woman in psychoanalytic theory, Mary Jacobus argues that gender identities, like words, are multiply significatory: "there is no 'proper' referent, male or female, only the masquerade of masculinity and femininity"; she sees "femininity itself" as the "betrayer," "the principle of difference" that must be "cast out" (15). "Femininity" itself is the subject of Sigmund Freud's late (1933) essay on female sexuality. Concerned with the social construction of woman—with the social construction of gender differences—Freud is, as de Lauretis notes in *Technologies of Gender*, one of the few theorists outside of feminist theory to conceive of a female subject. More commonly, in the work of Foucault, Althusser, Kristeva, for instance, "the terrain between sociality and subjectivity is one that leaves the female subject hopelessly caught in patriarchal swamps" (19). Not that psychoanalysis—or feminist theory—does not promote particular representations of gender grounded in sexual difference. Theory, too, is what neo-Marxist Louis Althusser would call an ideological state apparatus or what de Lauretis speaks of, following Foucault, as a "technology of gender." The construction of gender goes on, "if less obviously, in the academy, in the intellectual community, in avant-garde artistic practices and radical theories, even, and indeed especially, in feminism" (3).

If arguments for the essential nature of sexual difference are problematic, how can we "theorize gender beyond the limits of 'sexual difference' and the constraints that such a notion has come to impose on feminist critical thought" (ix)? Not unlike some feminisms, Freud represents femininity as, finally, an essential quality. However, his theory of the constitution of the *subject* is, as it is in my reading of Kroetsch's texts, more a narrative of the vacillation between subject positions than a fixing on one or the other. The vacillating positions of both the "woman" and the "man" in psychoanalytic theory are, like the positions of the speaking subject in the symbolic order, ex/positions, based on absence, lack, and desire. Another theorist of the cinema, Stephen Heath, suggests that twentieth-century Western culture has "produced sexuality as *the* meaning, including the meaning of feminism (thus equivalent to and contained within 'sexual liberation'), as a kind of natural-essence bedrock, what it's all about, where we really are" (19). We conceive of identity as based on an innate sexuality "where we really are." In "Sex and the Emergence of Sexuality," Arnold Davidson confronts what he sees as some "fundamental conceptual problems that get passed over imperceptibly when this topic [sexuality] is discussed" (16). Perhaps the fundamental conceptual problem lies in a failure to acknowledge that "sexuality" *is* a *conceptual* problem, not a natural phenomenon.

Acknowledging Foucault's *History of Sexuality* and a collection of essays edited by Philippe Ariès and André Béjin, Davidson traces the concept of "sexuality" to the nineteenth century: "although we take it to be a natural phenomenon, a phenomenon of nature not falling within the domain of historical emergence, our experience of sexuality is a product of systems of knowledge and modalities of power that bear no claim to ineluctability" (18). Contrary to a pre-nineteenth-century "experience of the flesh" (18) and an "anatomical style of reasoning" about sexual identity, Davidson finds in Freud and the "psychiatric style of reasoning" (25) a way to talk about sexual identity apart from anatomy and apart from gender.

As Davidson argues, Freud's theory of the psychic production of sexual desire would seem to offer us a theory of the social construction of sexual identity. Instead, since Freud, the concepts of "gender" and "sexuality" have become entirely confused with the concepts of "sex" and "anatomy." Consider *The Concise Oxford Dictionary* definitions. Both "anatomy," which signifies the "bodily structure of human beings," and "sex," "being male or female or hermaphrodite" speak of being human without binary sexual difference (*The Concise Oxford Dictionary*). When we move to the concepts of "gender" and "sexuality," however, binary difference is taken for granted. Tellingly, "gender" is defined as a "grammatical classification of objects *roughly* corresponding to *the two sexes* and sex*less*ness"; "sexuality" (not given its own entry but assumed under the meaning of "sexual") is "of sex, a sex, or the sexes; pertaining to relations *between the* sexes, esp. w. ref. to mutual attraction and to gratification of resulting desires" (italics added). Freud's essay on "Femininity" struggles with the possibility of a feminine sexual identity in the face of (so to speak—cf. Derrida; "What can look at itself is not one" [*Of Grammatology* 36]) the subject's difference from itself.

Chris Weedon rereads Freud this way: "in opposition to existing views of gender, childhood and sexuality, which saw gender identity as inborn and sexuality as an effect of puberty, Freud asserted that individuals were sexual beings from birth" (45). Freud makes a potentially more radical claim in "Femininity." Speaking initially of the findings of science on the subject of sexual identity, Freud's remarks have much wider implications:

> Portions of the male sexual apparatus also appear in women's bodies, though in an atrophied state, and, vice versa in the alternative case. It [science] regards their occurrence as indications of bisexuality, as though an individual is not a man or a woman but always both—merely a certain amount more the one than the other. (74)

To adapt this recognition of physical bisexuality to the psyche, one need only consider the sexual characteristics of the id. As Freud argues, infants are initially *neither* feminine nor masculine but "polymorphously perverse," finding pleasure in "oral, anal, and masturbatory forms of eroticism which in adults would be considered perversions" (*Dictionary of Psychology* 395).

Given the acknowledged polymorphously perverse state of infant sexuality, it would be more accurate to speak, not of original bisexuality (as Freud does repeatedly), but of sexuality as always already multi-sexual. We are all hermaphrodites, physically and psychologically. From birth, sexuality can be considered, not as a binary opposition, but as a play of relations. As Freud admits, from this polymorphously perverse state infants are "capable of developing either normal feminine or masculine identities *or neither*" (*An Outline of Psychoanalysis* 45; italics added). The concept of adult sexual identity as being "naturally" *either* masculine *or* feminine, of another identity as being a "perversion," is undercut by Freud's acknowledgement that identity is in fact "neither" one nor the other, "merely a certain amount *more* the one *than* the other" ("Femininity" 74).

I signal the entrance of the word "naturally" in the above sentence as an indication of the work of ideology—"the conscious or unconscious beliefs, habits, and social practices of a particular society. These often seem true, correct, and universal to members of that society, when in fact they are relative and specific to the society" (McCormick 285). As Althusser's work on the notion of ideology has suggested, although a particular code of behaviour comes to *seem* "natural," human activity (and human sexuality) is always culturally produced. Late twentieth-century ideology has been informed substantially by the assumptions that psychoanalysis has taught us to make about many things, including the family, sexuality, and femininity.

Although I would argue that psychoanalysis is Freud's explanation of how we come to be ("normal") sexualized selves or, neurotically, don't, what we speak of as "Freud's" theory is also always a reading of Freud's writings. With Derrida, I see psychoanalyatic theory as "a collection of texts belonging to my history and my culture" (*Of Grammatology* 160). Barry Cameron notes that Freudian analysis

> has been mistakenly invoked in support of sexism, biological determinism, and the bourgeois practice of analysis itself, especially American ego psychology, with attempts to integrate the individual into society as it is, based on an essentialist notion of a fixed, unchanging, transhistorical and transcultural self—that is, the Cartesian ego of liberal humanism that says that personality is determined by conscious subjectivity. (141)

Many other rereaders of Freud, including Jacques Lacan, Juliet Mitchell, Jacqueline Rose, Kaja Silverman, Jane Gallop, and Barry Cameron himself (though he would not entirely approve of that appellation) locate, in psychoanalytic theory, an undermining of traditional concepts of sexual difference. The question of sexual identity—how a "man" or a "woman" is constructed out of a polymorphously perverse infant—is, as Cameron notes, bound up with the question of the "individual." Male privilege is based on a repression of the "otherness" within the self. Nicole Brossard articulates the particularly lesbian feminist experience of difference within the subject when she writes: "within my own difference I see clearly" (40).

Consider the interrogation of the psychoanalytic explanation of identity founded in loss, absence, and difference in the following passage from Kroetsch's "The Poet's Mother":

....
In the death of my mother
I say good-bye to myself.
....
In the death of my mother
I recite my name.
(*Advice to My Friends* 139-40)

Or in the following passage:

In the snapshot my mother is seventeen.
She is standing beside an empty chair.
Today is my birthday, I am fifty-six.
I seat myself in the empty chair.

in the snapshot.
(*Advice to My Friends* 132)

Clearly "I" arises out of a recognition of the absence of the (m)other. "I" can only recite "my name" by losing "myself" as other. My self is a "self-portrait," a "found object, given name by another, appropriated." Like the concept of subjectivity as ex-centric (not centred in the self), like the recognition of polymorphous perversity in the infant, the Oedipus Complex problematizes Freud's theory of bisexuality, for it sublimates multiplicity in sexual identity to singular "hom(m)o-sexual" desire: "the little girl is," Freud says we are obliged to recognize, "a little man" (78). Lacan complicates the point when he reminds us that the little man is "l'hommelette"—scrambled, unidentifiable. In the most rigorous sense, the pre-Oedipal child is, like an omelet, a shapeless mass. Freud's narrative of human sexuality can be read therefore as a narrative of a desire for "male" sexuality (in the sense of self-presence) that, in language, can never be achieved. The position of the father is "one" never held. The desire to *take the place of* the father and to make love to (and inscribe) the mother (Kroetsch: "In this poem I rehearse my mother. / I hold the snapshot in my hands. / I become her approaching lover" [*Advice to My Friends* 132])—the Oedipal crisis—describes *the* situation (and the situatedness) of the subject: "These are the scars / that make us whole" (142). In effect, the Oedipal crisis never "passes"; we each remain more or less or neither masculine or feminine.

Consider, for instance, that to resolve the Oedipal crisis, the male child must appropriate an image of his father. In doing so he must resolve his feelings of jealousy and desire (in the sense of wanting to take the place of, wanting an end to wanting, an end to difference, to metaphor, to language) for his father. But the identification is a complex one: the child not only identifies with the father; "he" must also accept that there are ways in which he can never *be* the father (he too must be a not-he, a she): "he" can only be like (a) him. He can only play at being a man. In other words, while the male subject internalizes an image of the father, he also internalizes his own difference from his father, his loss of a never-held position, his real lack of phallic authority. The concept of "the father," like the concept of difference, is both the point at which the son's desires are made possible and the agency by which they are forever deferred.

Freud argues that the "girl child" (itself an odd configuration, assuming an already-constituted sexual identity in a child as yet to be identified), who never can appropriate an image of the father, remains stuck in the Oedipus Complex, never fully forming a superego. But, as I have just argued, neither does the "male" child. To (want to) be the father is to be different: "the phallus can only take up its place by indicating the precariousness of any identity assumed by the subject on the basis of its token" (Mitchell 40). The "subject" comes into being only out of and through an awareness of this lack and insufficiency: as subjects we are all "women."

In his discussion of feminine sexuality Freud asked what has become a notorious question: "What do women want?" My argument suggests that this question applies to both men and women. As Juliet Mitchell has also argued, the answer, in either case, is simply that both women and men *want—that* is the human condition (24): "to be human is to be subjected to a law which decentres and divides: sexuality is created in a division, the subject is split" (Mitchell 26). To be constituted as a "subject" in a patriarchal society is to be subjected to perpetual lack and therefore to desire: "to desire an end to desire / is to desire" (Kroetsch, *Advice to My Friends* 65).

As Mitchell notes, the concept of the split subject derives from Freud's vocabulary of differences within. Rather than a unified, stable, male self, Freud constructs the psychic apparatus as a network where "each part acquires its specificity from a distinct signifying system'' (Silverman 51). The ego is subjected to both the id's biological drives and the superego's social pressures. If its ideal function is to satisfy simultaneously the demands of the id, of the superego, and of reality, this reconciliation of conflicting demands is never completely accomplished. The ego exists at the crossroads of the three pressures and is in a state of perpetual conflict. As Kroetsch would say, ''We are each our own crossroads.'' It is Freud's explanation of the human person as split that gives me a way to talk about the decentred subject which (dis)appears in the Kroetschian text as a(-)woman. ''I'' is a character whose existence is constituted at the crossroads of so many demands and pressures that it cannot be seen as a fixed point but as a continually changing, or decentred, process.

My reading of Kroetsch's writing is like my reading of psychoanalytic theory in that I find there a theory of difference which sees differences within subjectivity. ''One'' (as many) can acknowledge a range of places from which to speak, many ways of being for each ''I'': ''Identity . . . is at once impossible and unavoidable'' (Kroetsch, *Excerpts* 15). These ''impossible and unavoidable'' places exist across the spectrum of sexual differences, without the opposition male/female, against the fixed consciousness of the logocentric metaphysics of presence. Chapters Three to Eight locate the many forms of resistance to the phallogocentric universe in Kroetsch's texts, from Anna Dawe's rewriting of her ''father's'' field notes to Demeter's rewriting of Hazard's story. I go now to Kroetsch's ''deliberate playground'' (Jamal ''Acknowledgements'').

PART TWO

Reading Kroetsch

The world does not end. It's hard to make a literature out of that realization. But at least the father disappears. And that, out west (as opposed to down east), makes everything possible.

—Kroetsch, "The Disappearing Father and Harrison's Born-Again and Again West"

CHAPTER THREE

Rereading *Field Notes*: *Badlands* and the Continuing Poem

> I don't know that I ever received a letter from my absent father. He sent us instead, left us, deposited for me to find, his field notes.
>
> —*Badlands*

> [Anna Dawe's] gift is her ability to "untell" while telling, to tell a story while assaulting that story, to mediate (& she calls herself a "mediator") between naming and unnaming. She is able to adopt a certain ambivalence, the "borderline" stance of the Kroetschian artist figure.
>
> —Jeanette Seim

> And the congenial form for Kroetsch's most feminist novel is field notes.
>
> —Laurie Ricou

If, as Laurie Ricou argues in an entry in *A Mazing Space*, Kroetsch's most feminist novel is written in the form of field notes, to which "field notes" is he referring? *Badlands* or *Field Notes*? Moreover, are the challenges to assumptions about meaning, coherence, and intention which a text of field notes works from feminist? I begin by attending to the possibilities of meaning—to the differences that are telling—with/in the words "field" and "notes." With Kroetsch, I see words as "intersection[s] where things can happen. In a sense writers are forever misreading words" (*Labyrinths of Voice* 149). Because *The Oxford English Dictionary* includes, among the range of meanings of "field," both ground and a piece of ground, one could argue that (the) "field" is both replete and fragmented. "Notes" are also both a record of facts *written* down—notes are writings—and explanatory or critical annotations or comments added to a passage in a writing (supplementary readings). Which field notes are feminist? Which field notes is Kroetsch writing? In this chapter I read at the crossroads, among, between, and within at least two of the meanings of field notes, and the two pieces of writing which appropriate the field notes form.

In an unlikely feminist gesture, Anna Dawe writes that "women are not supposed to have stories." But her words immediately betray her: like her father William Dawe, Anna, too, is a teller of tales who feels it is "left" to her to "mediate the story" (*Badlands* 3). Her mediation of the story is a deconstruction of male privilege. Although Dawe (the father) seems to occupy *the* patriarchal position, not only as father, but as "originator and financier" (8), as someone who is "not looking for fragments, I want a complete and total specimen" (155), Anna's narrative glosses on her father's field notes, the unnaming as naming which constitutes *Badlands*, and points out that her father's story was always already (a) "her" story. What remains of Dawe's search for truth is his daughter's story, her recognition that, although "the occasion would demand of her a formal telling, would sponsor the curious little tricks of a male adventure. . . . They have their open spaces and translate them into a fabled hunting" (27). The "tricks of male adventure," the tricks of narrative, both conceal and reveal the lack of totality: "total and absurd male that he was, he assumed, like a male author, an omniscience that was not ever his, a scheme that was not ever there" (76). Anna reads her father's notes to point out that history was always capable of being read as (a) her story.

As I am attempting to do with Kroetsch's, Anna both does, and undoes, a feminist critique of her father's writing. Like her father, "she" is inscribed as an "I" on a most unstable site—the site of her father's citations: "Because in the sun by the river, reading in my father's field books, we began to look at those abrupt notes as he had looked at his prized skeletons, wondering and wondering" (258). Her identity is both posited, and immediately called into question. As author "she" speaks, but her words tell us that "she" does not have the "omniscience that was not ever his." Neither does the reader of *Field Notes*. *Badlands* teaches us how to misread *Field Notes*.

Kroetsch describes *Field Notes* as "an autobiographical poem, one in which I just cannot accept any of the conventions of autobiography." Writing "I" in unconventional autobiography can "free us from self . . . from the humanistic temptation to coerce the world" (*Labyrinths* 208-209):

> he is a manifestation
> of I
> but haven't we met.
>
> (*Field Notes* 88)

Like Kroetsch, Shirley Neuman suggests that the "field" of *Field Notes* is an autobiographical field, an archaeological site on which the self is constructed (*Labyrinths* 207). Kroetsch:

> My own continuing poem is called, somewhat to my dismay, *Field Notes*. Perhaps Olson's field is there somewhere, but more specifically I think of the field notes kept by the archaeologist, by the finding man, the finding man who is essentially lost. . . . There might, that is, be a hidden text. Yet, it is as if we spend our lives finding clues, fragments, shards, leading or misleading details, chipped tablets written over in a forgotten language. ("For Play and Entrance" 103)

If the "self" is *found*ed *on* and *as* an archaeological site/cite, in fragments, shards, leading or misleading details, it will be necessarily incomplete. The finding man (the "I" who finds himself/a man) is "essentially lost." The poet as archaeologist is the naming "man" who is essentially unnamed and then renamed "woman" by/in writing.

Kroetsch's "story" of growing up in Alberta, seeing what his father called "buffalo wallows" and not finding anyone educated who had heard of them, suggested to him that history (which was not his story) could not account for the world he lived in. Because the "authorized history, the given definition of history," was betraying him on the prairies, Kroetsch turned to the model of archaeology:

> the prairie writer understands the appropriateness [of the archaeological model] in terms of the particulars of place: newspaper files, place names, shoe boxes full of old photographs, tall tales, diaries, journals, tipi rings, weather reports, business ledgers, votary records. ("On Being an Alberta Writer" 76)

The field notes kept by the prairie "archaeologist" Kroetsch are, like Anna Dawe's father's notes, "found" pieces. Like the archaeologist's artifacts, our words are always already left for us. In a patriarchy, they are always already our "father's" words.

Like Kroetsch, Anna and I are left with notes from the field, field notes, written by different kinds of "fathers." In a sense we are all constructed out of our readings of various field notes. As Eli Mandel suggests in his introduction to *Field Notes*, the "field" is the "place" of writing/of having been written:

> where (how) it grows, where it dies, where it takes place: ground, open field, field force, field games, the place defined in its telling. The double place of self and other, body and spirit, man and woman. The double voice of that comic spiller of tales or speller of kells or teller of spills. The antiphonal endless story of love and death, truth and lies. Each story, in other words (and there are always other words), tells another story. The poem is continuing because it cannot end. (7)

As Anna does, I (literally) "find myself" lost with "his" *Field Notes*.

With Anna, I read the field notes which, like all our words, are left by an absent "father." Like Anna, I speak (of) "his" words "to set straight the record" (*Badlands* 45) while recognizing that "the" record was never there, "his" words were never "his." "Home"—a woman's word—is a word that (a) "he" understands:

> Home was a word he understood, and heroes cannot afford that understanding. Which meant he must become a fool among those fools.
>
> Or so I would assume, from reading the field notes: and I allow, generously, for my father's weariness at the end of a long day, for his sinking ambition. . . . Action and voice: how strange they should have so little connection. Or is there any at all, any familiar knock at the closed door, between the occurrence and the most exact telling. . . .
>
> There are no truths, only correspondences. (*Badlands* 45)

As Anna does, I see only correspondence(s) (he *did* send letters after all) in the (textual) place of truth.

In one sense, *Badlands* is not written like *Field Notes* at all. *Badlands* is already a daughter's deconstruction of her *father's* field notes. "His" field notes have already been read. In Kroetsch's *Field*

Notes I have only (the?) notes; "I" do the reading that Anna performs in *Badlands*. I re/form my father. I *re*gather the "pieces" left on this archaeological site (*Field Notes*)—"pieces" like his *Stone Hammer Poems, The Ledger, Seed Catalogue*—and find that in language our catalogues are always dispersing (they *are* "seed" catalogues), our words, our collections, can only name absences:

> the absence of silk worms
> the absence of clay and wattles (whatever the hell they are)
> the absence of Lord Nelson
> the absence of kings and queens
> the absence of a bottle opener, and me with a
> vicious attack of
> the absence of both Sartre and Heidegger. (54)

One could, of course, go on (in language one does!). Words can only name absences, other words which are themselves absent. It is this absence of words which is played with obsessively in Kroetsch's writing, which teases us with the possibility that without words there are no things; without the story you cannot "grow a poet." Like the archaeologist, the poet "can give twenty names and only hope that the nameless thing has been recognized by that": "Dawe, furiously, in the outrageous silence of his writing trying to cite or fashion or penetrate or plumb or receive or accomplish or postulate or pretend the absolute truth that would give him his necessary lie" (*Badlands* 239).

Kroetsch's attention to the problem of naming has a parallel in feminist theory. For much Anglo-American feminism, the "nameless thing" (like Kroetsch's "buffalo wallows") is "female experience" or (problematically, if we recall Lacan's crossing out of the "the") the "woman's perspective." By giving "twenty" or more names to what are regarded as pre-existent "things"—"female" things—they hope to be recognized. But the very *plurality* of names itself indicates that the "nameless thing" becomes "recognized" only by and as more deferred namings: "secretly at night I turn signs around, I point / all travelers in the wrong direction; I've so far / derailed three trains; I look at bridges malignantly" (*Field Notes* 111).

In a passage which addresses the liberal feminist desire to give names to "her" experience Kroetsch writes, "at one time I considered it the task of the Canadian writer to give names to his experience, to be the namer. I now suspect that on the contrary, it is his task to un-name" ("Unhiding the Hidden" 17). Both the task of naming, of affirming presence (and, within a patriarchal economy, legitimacy), and of unnaming, of deconstructing (bastardizing) or undermining the metaphysics of presence are obsessions in Robert Kroetsch's work. But Kroetsch's desire to name, "to make up a story. Our story" ("On Being an Alberta Writer"), is always doubled by the awareness that language is *not* a transparent medium; if there is a "real" (world) to speak of, it is (a, the) fiction that makes it, and us.

In the long poems included as *Field Notes*, the desire to name and to unname is complicated by a third tendency: the desire to rename. A better triad of words might be construct, destruct, and deconstruct, for, as Barbara Johnson notes,

> The very word deconstruction is meant to undermine the either/or logic of the opposition "construction/destruction." Deconstruction is both, it is neither, and it reveals the way in which both construction and destruction are themselves not what they appear to be. (*A World of Difference* 12)

Homologously, "naming" and "unnaming" are not what they appear to be either; each is traversed by the other. As Jeanette Seim notes, Anna Dawe's "gift is her ability to 'untell' while telling, to tell a story while assaulting that story, to mediate (& she calls herself a 'mediator') between naming and unnaming." Kroetsch's activity in writing is simultaneously a deconstruction and a reconstruction. When he "names" *The Ledger*, for instance, he finds that it is both something fixed—"A book that lies permanently in some place"—and unfixable—"A book that lies / permanently."

"The Silent Poet Eats His Words" is a poem which renames the cliché by offering metonymic associations: "whatever you do, don't," or "the penny saved is, generally, lost; a stitch in time seams nothing, ha" (112). In rewriting the cliché, in "eating" others' (our fathers') words—which we find ourselves always already speaking—the poet exploits the semantic possibilities of any word, of any "self" which is found (in) speaking. Hannah Arendt writes (in words that link intertextually with Kroetsch through their appearance in *Labyrinths of Voice* 168) that for Walter Benjamin, "to quote is to name." But if all our words are quotations, there is no original context, no moment of origin for the word (not even on the prairies). Every sign can be cited, put between quotation marks. The poet does not name in the sense of making new or originating; s/he quotes.

The narrator in "The Sad Phoenician" recognizes this condition of language when he says "I am, you might say, a kind of Phoenician, with reference, that is, to my trading in language, even in, to stretch the point, my being at sea" (79). Like the sad Phoenician we, too, are at sea with Kroetsch's poems which ask us to "tow" the "line," to make our own notes on the field. George Bowering asks, in "Stone Hammer Narrative," "'Field Notes'. . . . How do I do that? I can field a pop-up pretty well, and a grounder as long as it is hit right at me. I can field questions if I'm cornered or paid. But how do you field notes?" (131). All I can do, after George Bowering, is begin by mixing my metaphors once more and playing Kroetsch's game with him. The words which follow are a narrative of my fieldings of Kroetsch's *Notes*, particularly his "Sketches of a Lemon."

This Is Not a Lemon

"Sketches of a Lemon" questions the possibility of producing presence in writing, and, analogously, the possibility of maintaining a fixed or singular identity in words. *The Concise Oxford Dictionary* defines the word sketch: "a preliminary, rough, slight, merely outlined, or unfinished drawing or painting often as an experiment for or to assist in the making of a regular picture." But a sketch is also a writing: a "brief account without many details conveying the general idea of something, a rough draft, a general outline." In a section of *Autobiography* dedicated to Robert Kroetsch, bpNichol points out the metaphor at work in our speaking of a sketch or a writing as a "draft": "a draft he calls it. Like it blew in through a crack in the mind. Just a bunch of hot air" ("The Lungs: A Draft" 45). Although the sketch tries to name—it tells you some*thing*—it simultaneously unnames—it tells the difference. The multiple meanings of the word "sketch" signify both the incompleteness and doubleness of representation.

Like Derrida's concept of erasure, the sketch achieves a suspension of concepts by invoking a word and then placing an invisible "X" through it. As the speaker in "The Sad Phoenician" says, "X marks the known, the spot where she was / but isn't" (82). Christopher Norris writes, "the mark of erasure acknowledges both the inadequacy of the terms employed—their highly provisional status—and the fact that thought simply cannot manage without them" (69):

> even the Virgin Queen, she wasn't
> Shakespeare either
> But I did scorn them all, she wrote
> and with good cause: a leman is a lemon, ha;
> well, let the heads fall.
> ("The Silent Poet at Intermission" 108)

Is "a leman is a lemon" a cross-linguistic pun? Is "le/man" (the man) a lemon? How *do* you grow a lemon except by fielding it, by planting it in a linguistic field?

The lemon is not furnished or finished by/in the twelve sketches. The line "so much for that," which is repeated, like a refrain, throughout the "lament" (or should I say "lemont") for this lemon, articulates the futility of trying to re-present things in words. Perhaps this poem—in fact each poem in the *Field Notes* collection—could be re-named "this is not a lemon." "Sketches of a Lemon" reminds us that whenever we *write* a word (the word "man," say) our words are always already telling us that "this is not a man."

I think of René Magritte's painting, "Ceci n'est pas une pipe," in which the words present on the canvas invoke only the absence of things. Like an "X," the words "Ceci n'est pas une pipe" are, in the Magritte work, written over a photographic realist representation of a pipe. The presence of text on canvas suggests at least two levels of signification. Although the sketched and painted metaphor for the pipe resembles a pipe and signifies that it is a pipe, the layer of this palimpsestic work which offers us words (and, presumably, meaning) points out that what we see is not, and can never be, the pipe itself (we *are* at "sea," ha!).

Moreover, the demonstrative pronoun "ceci" (the possible cross-linguistic pun for the English reader—"this see/sea"—merely reinforces the instability of the signifier) *tells* us that the word "ceci" is not the word "pipe." Magritte's painting addresses the problems of representation in any medium: there is always a gap not only between signifier and signified but also between sign systems and the things to which, supposedly, they refer, between the name and the continuum of experiences which our sign systems *tell* us are "there."

"Sketches of a Lemon" is, in this sense, not even a series of sketches of lemons. It is words about words about words. The signifier never refers directly to the signified because *both* signifier and signified are constructed and arbitrarily linked. Shirley Neuman explains:

> While the sign asserts an (arbitrary) link between "tree" and the concept of that plant out there on the lawn, in fact one can only explain the signifier "tree" by further signs. One gets into an endless regression, an endless renaming. At the same time as one asserts a link, one is also asserting analogy and disunity. (*Labyrinths* 92)

So too for lemons. As Kroetsch's poem haltingly begins: "A lemon is almost round. /Some lemons are almost round. /A lemon is not round" (123). The lemon is "named" ("it" is almost round), unnamed (only some lemons are almost round so not all lemons are round), and renamed (a lemon is not round; it must have an *other* name; the poem must continue). As Kroetsch writes at the end of the first edition of *Seed Catalogue*, "readers are invited to compose further sections."

In Part 2 the poet looks, as Anna does in *Badlands*, to his (?) father's words (literally!) and to another kind of father's words—the literary tradition—for a way to speak (of) lemons. S/he finds not identification, metaphor, but difference, metonomy: "As my father used to say / well I'll be cow-kicked / by a mule. / He was especially fond of lemon meringue pie" (123). Because the poet's father and lemons are metonymically linked—"He was especially fond / of lemon meringue pie"—the poet hopes for an answer to the question—how do you grow a lemon? Such is not the case: "To go from metaphor to metonymy is to go from the temptation of the single to the allure of multiplicity. Instead of the temptations of "origins' we have the genealogies that multiply our connections into the past, into the world" (Kroetsch, *Labyrinths of Voice* 117).

The writer's frustrated sense of belatedness, of never *having* the thing itself, of having only others' words (field notes, or letters, in all senses), is suggested in Part 3: "I went and looked at Francis Ponge's poem / on blackberries. If blackberries can be / blackberries, I reasoned, by a kind of analogy, / lemons can, I would suppose, be lemons. / Such was not the case" (124). Again, the inevitable failure of the mimetic attempt—this poem is not this lemon—is articulated. I am reminded of Professor Mark Madham's "letter" to Miss Jill Sunderman at the beginning of *Gone Indian*: "At the end of your letter you ask me, in your offhand manner, to 'explain everything.' Let me reply that I feel under no obligation to explain anything" (1).

As readers we—like the "I" of this poem—are, like Jill Sunderman ("she" too is divided within, a "sunder-man"), seeking to have everything explained. But all we receive are letters signed by "Mark." As Derrida argues, "by definition, a written signature implies the actual or empirical nonpresence of the signer. But, it will be said, it also marks and retains his having been present in a past now, which will remain a future now and therefore in a now in general, in the transcendental form of nowness (*maintenance*)" ("Signature Event Context" 329). But, as for Derrida, so too for Kroetsch: it is the "disruption of presence in the mark, what here I am calling writing" (327)—"Mark" is a "Mad-ham"—that delights.

If Kroetsch signs "his" letters—if he is writing autobiography—it is with a "post-Mark" in a "post-age" when the "real" is always provisional. In these poems there is no "one" (unified self) to "receive" letters, no "one" message available to be sent. As this poem insists, in wanting to speak of lemons, one continually speaks (of/in) metaphor, difference—what lemons are not:

> Sketches, I reminded myself,
> not of a pear, not of an apple nor of a peach
> nor of . . .
> the usual bunch of grapes,
> fresh from the vine,
> just harvested, glistening with dew.
>
> (124)

Although naming consists of (indeed insists upon) absence, not presence, the naming functions only by simultaneously asserting the presence and absence of a real world and a constructed one, a speaking voice and a spoken one: "Smaro, I called, I'm hungry" (124).

Part 5 of the poem moves, by analogy, away from the lemon and asks the question "what about oranges" (125). This six-line "sketch" unnames itself by repeating the word "oranges" at the end of five of the six lines. Here the subject is lack of subject: "most oranges bear a remarkable resemblance / to oranges" (125). Kroetsch discusses the problem of lack of subject in *Labyrinths of Voice*: "If we have nothing to write about, but nothing to write about, that is what we have to write about. We go right back to the naming act in a radical sense; we are in Adam's position with no beasts out there, we even have to invent the beasts" (144). This poem says instead that "this poem is about nothing," or rather, words, as Eli Mandel might have said, in the sense that the orange referred to in the poem is "nothing" but the word "orange" in the poem: "an orange / looks like an orange. / In fact, most oranges / bear a remarkable resemblance / to oranges" (125).

Part 6 makes a narrative attempt at accessing the lemon: "Smaro is rolling a lemon on the breadboard. / The breadboard is flat, horizontal, is motionless. / The lemon rolls back and forth on the motionless surface" and so on. But more than an attempt at situating, at contextualizing if you like, the lemon, goes on here: there is also a rolling back and forth of the syntax and of the possibilities of meaning in the phrases. First the "lemon rolls back and forth" then "Smaro's hand moves back and forth." At first "Smaro is rolling a lemon" and then the "lemon rolls" itself. The surface, that is, the syntax and the semantics of the poem, is not motionless, named, but contradictory, in a state of perpetual unnaming and renaming.

The poet's relation to the object desired, or rather, the relation between language and the object of desire, is played with in Part 7:

> I had a very strong desire
> to kiss a lemon.
> No one was watching.
> I kissed a lemon.
>
> So much for that.

Does my desire for the lemon, my linguistic "kissing" of a lemon in a poem, make the lemon present? No; "so much for that." Desire is endless. Even when we say we have the object of desire (the poet "kissed *the* lemon") our saying makes it absent. In Part 8, not saying, too, invokes only absence: "I bought a second-hand car— / Okay, okay." But the joke is on the poet. It is the reader who has the space on the page to fill in the word "lemon" after line 1 while the poet imposes closure with the words "Okay, okay."

In response to the question, "If someone asked me, / how is a lemon shaped?" the poet offers three open-ended fragments in

Part 9: "(the salmon / (the oven / (the lemon." The reader is invited to produce a linear narrative out of the words. For example, we could say that the lemon was squeezed onto the salmon in the oven and left for an hour (although that would be pretty awful salmon) and in that way the lemon is "shaped" (that is, determined by such a narrative) "exactly like an hour." The reader might choose instead to see the three words as only differentially related. The word "salmon" is not the word "oven" because, although they share the "o" and the "n" and their last syllables rhyme, the "salmon" has the "sal" (a pun on "salle?" room) and the oven doesn't. Is the "oven" not the lemon because it doesn't have an "l" and an "m" even though it does have the "o," "e," and the "n"? Who knows, One way or the other (and there are always other ways), a parenthetical voice tells us, "Now we're getting somewhere" (126). Indeed, the continuing poem is always "getting" and "begetting" but never arrives.

The poet of the "lemon cure" in Part 10 is the healer or trickster or shaman:

> The lemon cure.
> In each glass
> mix: 1 stick cinnamon
>   1 teaspoon honey
>   2 cloves
>   2 jiggers rum
>   1/2 slice lemon
>   hot water to taste
> Repeat as necessary.

The poem as recipe seems to offer us (finally) a real (at least a practical) relation between language and the world. But, as Kroetsch acknowledges, the poet as trickster is often tricked himself: "There is no logic to his behaviour, or only anti-logic" (*Labyrinths* 99); "He's very subversive, very carnivalesque" (100). To offer this kind of found lemon poem is to say, this is where the lemon was, but is not.

Part 11 could be read as an attempt to ritually chant the lemon into existence. But the "poem for a child who has just bitten into / a halved lemon that has just been squeezed" works not only by the voice and the sound, by the repetition of the words "see, what did I tell you," but also by being present as writing, as a pattern of words on the page:

see, what did I tell you, see
what did I tell you, see, what
did I tell you, see, what did
I tell you, see, what did I
tell you, see, what did I tell
you, see, what did I tell you

These words can be read linearly or vertically. As the last line of the poem says, "One could, of course, go on." But these are only words. In an important sense, we can never "see" what we are "told." The things I "tell" you are, by definition, absent from your seeing. You are at sea.

The final part moves from the narrative "I" to the first person plural "we"—presumably referring to the poet and "Smaro," but again, who knows.

This hour is shaped like
a lemon. We taste its light

on the baked salmon.
The tree itself is elsewhere.

We make faces, liking the
sour surprise. Our teeth melt.

We return to the image of the lemon "shaped" like an hour, or at least we think we do, until we recall that the metaphor has been reversed. Now the hour is shaped like a lemon. In poems, all one can say is that things themselves are (like the origin of the lemon—the tree) always "elsewhere." This final, but inconclusive, part of the poem works by unlikely metaphorical and rhythmic juxtaposition: the hour like the lemon, the sour surprise, the teeth that melt. But again, these are fragments, mixed metaphors, notes, not definitions. Like the long poem *Field Notes*, these metaphors evade as much as they suggest about meaningfulness.

Perhaps the concept of "renaming" can be replaced with the concept of "retelling." After all, Kroetsch is not only concerned with "naming," in the sense of positing a new set of real beasts in a real world. He is also concerned with "telling" stories—stories about words about stories about stories about words about words that always tell more than they can say. This is the kind of practice that makes a poem continue, that makes a continuing poem a juxtaposition of both the present as nameable and the present as an absence which is, finally, unnameable. To what Samuel Beckett wrote in *The Unnameable*, "I'm in words, made of words, others' words" (386) Kroetsch would agree, but with the rejoinder that, as he writes in the last poem in another continuation of the continuing poem, *Advice to My Friends*—to which I shall return—called, in "telling" fashion, "envoi (to begin with)":

There is no real
world, my friends.
Why not, then,
let the stars
shine in our bones?

As I have noted, the Acknowledgements page of Ashraf Jamal's provocative master's thesis on Kroetsch's writing includes a thank-you to his supervisor—Barry Cameron (another astute reader of Kroetsch)—for "taking" him to "Kroetsch's deliberate playground." I appropriate the uncannily appropriate phrase to suggest that, like *Field Notes* and *Badlands*, all of Kroetsch's texts ask to be read as cites/sites of and at play. They are deliberately poststructuralist texts. But their poststructuralist aspects—the undermining of representation, exploitation of the plurality of meaning in words, the plurality of sexuality in identity—are also feminist strategies in that they cajole us into rereading our concepts of so-called "male" identity as always already traversed by the other.

As examples of *écriture féminine* in the most radical senses of those words, Kroetsch writes as a "post-man" (Gregory Ulmer's words for Jacques Derrida) whose "letters bear a message that never arrives," whose "message" is the impossibility of transferring messages, whose words articulate a theory that, in its overturning of signifier and signified, male and female, self and other, excerpts and the real world, participates in that doubled practice which allows us, as subjects of our own agency, to make differences even while those differences make us.

For Kroetsch, as for Freud, Derrida, Kristeva, and de Lauretis, "man," as a stable position in opposition to "woman," must, like the self, be seen as "questionable." Like my identity, my sexual identity is both subject to question and unquestionable. "I" speak "as a woman" only by shifting continually between and within many discursive positions, each of which, at a given moment, allows me access to particular ways of being. But it is precisely because the subject does speak from these multiple points, because there are so many productively contradictory discursive sites on which we can and do play, that, happily, sexual identity can be seen as more multiple and vacillating than we often believe. As the narrator in a poem by George Bowering self-consciously notes in a passage Kroetsch includes as epigraph to a recent addition of his continuing poem:

> We all live in the same world's sea. We cannot tell a story that leaves us outside, and when I say we, I include you. But in order to include you, I feel I cannot spend these pages saying I to a second person. Therefore let us say *he*, and stand together looking at them. ("Spending the Morning on the Beach")

In light of the feminist reading practice *Badlands* and *Field Notes* teach, I turn now from the later poetry to a first novel, *But We Are Exiles*, published in 1965.

CHAPTER FOUR

Exposing the Subject: The Line in (the) Peter's Hand(s): Or, *But We Are Exiles*

"One day—out there on the prairies in a small farmers' town—I sat down and filled out a postcard. . . . The message ran on so I bought another card, and then I needed another, and all this little café had was cards with pictures on them of rabbits as big as horses and potatoes four or five to a wagon-load. And pretty soon I had thirteen cards covered."

"But I didn't get them."

"I only had stamps for a few. Four or five maybe."

"But I didn't get any, Pete. Never. None."

"I don't believe I mailed them."

—*But We Are Exiles*

I just want the simple facts. The bare unvarnished facts to send to the head office.

—*But We Are Exiles*

There are thus two interpretations of interpretation, of structure, of sign, of freeplay. The one seeks to decipher, dreams of deciphering, a truth or an origin which is free from freeplay and from the order of the sign, and lives like an exile the necessity of interpretation. The other, which is no longer turned toward the origin, affirms freeplay and tries to pass beyond man and humanism, the name man being the name of that being who, throughout . . . his history—has dreamed of full presence, the reassuring foundation, the origin and the end of game.

—Derrida, "Structure, Sign, and Play in the Discourse of the Human Sciences," in Macksey and Donato

Fair these broad meads—these hoary woods are grand,
But we are exiles from our fathers' land.

—Refrain to the "Canadian Boat-Song" 1892

What interpretation of interpretation does *But We Are Exiles* make? Is it a piece of writing which re-affirms the possibility of "full presence, the reassuring foundation, the origin and the end of game"? Is it a classic realist text which is in search of "the simple facts"? Or does it do both simultaneously by making its readers inquire into the implications of writing supplementary postcards and being unable, finally, to send—or to receive—them? Are we exiles when we run away from home, or are we always already exiles "at home" (*chez-soi*—in the self)? I consider explicitly the double play of self/other, here/there, subject/agent in this reading of *But We Are Exiles*.

Certainly many readers of *But We Are Exiles*, including Peter Thomas and Russell Brown, do not find a rehearsal of the kind of meta-fictional, meta-autobiographical play that we have come to expect in Kroetsch's recent work. Although it is possible to read *But We Are Exiles* as simply a classic realist text, part of the agenda I have set for myself is to recognize that you never can tell. . . . As Robert Lecker notices, "As soon as Kroetsch seduces us into believing that his first novel is traditional, he signals his struggle with that tradition" (23). Lecker tells us that Kroetsch "tells us that in writing *Exiles*": "I aimed at . . . what would look like a simple reliable surface. . . . Then you begin to suspect what lies beneath it. I want to have both those things operating, both that clinging to day that we have, and yet that awareness of a tremendous undertow" (92). I read *But We Are Exiles* as an exposition of what "lies" beneath the surface. The subject of the text is the agent in the text. Always already constituted in exile from "his" (liberal humanist) "self," the male subject, Peter Guy, is both "holding" and "running" from the line: looking in the mirror and playing at being a man.

The text of *But We Are Exiles* seems to open with a realist, third-person narrator posited as storyteller: "The line in Peter's hands came taut just then" (1). Although the "line" in this line could be a fishing line, at this moment of reading I am not sure. As the slippage of the line in the line I have just written indicates, the text has begun to tell on itself in quite provocative ways. Unlike the omniscience and confidence of the classic realist narrator, there just may be a "self"-conscious "I" speaking/writing *these* lines. The "line" in "Peter's" hand(s) could be the line in/on which (the) Peter is written, on which Peter "writes." Reading this early text through Kroetsch's later texts can teach us to produce such playful misreadings. This opening sentence can tell us that language does not unproblematically and transparently reproduce "reality," as the classic realist text has traditionally assumed. Writing always say more and differently than the author intends—or not.

The first page of *But We Are Exiles* suggests a recognition that Kroetsch comes to in his later work: that, as Mieke Bal argues, in a third-person narrative, "I" and "he" are both "I" (121). The words "I narrate" are always prefixed to any seemingly omniscient third-person narrative. We could read the opening lines this way: "[I narrate:] The line in Peter's hands came taut just then; a chill shuddered up into his arms and aching neck. [I narrate] He heard himself yell" (3). This narrating subject, in her absent presence, may have struggled with, revised, and rewritten this first "line" of text: the "line" *does* become "taut" just at the moment it is *re*read. There is an exploitation of the difference between the agent who writes and the subject who appears in the discourse of the text; between the Peter of the line and the Peter holding the line.

Consider the name of this contradictory figure: Peter Guy. As a euphemism for the male phallus, "Peter" is not only divided but possibly feminized; if "he" is *not* "*him*self" could he be a "her"? "He heard himself yell" indicates that there is a difference between the "he" who speaks and the "he" who listens to the speaking. Like the Lacanian subject whose identity is formed only out of an awareness of lack—of the difference *within* the speaking subject—the subject of/in this text experiences identity as a perpetual mirror stage:

> He glanced up at the breath-tripping hush; at the broad river, mirror-smooth in the afternoon sun. . . . He looked down again at the water and this time he saw his own face watching him. . . . He studied the reflection as if not sure whom he might see. (2)

Although it seems to offer a stable and coherent self, the mirror which, as Kroetsch says in *Labyrinths*, "makes things backwards again" (187), is always breakable: "The image mimicked his hesitation, mocked his doubt by repeating it. . . . Peter shook his head to be sure it was himself he saw. A drop of water from the rising line scarred his face, exploded his frail composure" (2). The "face" we think of as our own is, like Mike Hornyak's at the end of *But We Are Exiles*, "broken" (145).

The words of the title suggest that because we appropriate our "father's" land/words/self "we" are never ourselves. The narrator of "Stone Hammer Poem" recognizes that the poem being written is like the stone maul which "was found. // In the field / my grandfather / thought / was his // my father / thought was his" (*Field Notes* 14). Like mirrors, our words exile us from ourselves:

> Peter walked into her room . . . looked in on a mirror and the image of two raging bodies, a tumble of dark hair. And he was caught. He fled and fled and was caught there trapped, doomed in that long mahogany frame. He fled and went on searching and could not see himself. (145)

Flee as we might, we *are* caught; we have no "stable" (there is no room at the inn; no inn-er self to find) self to "see," to go "home" to. We are exiles because we are caught simultaneously in front of and within the mirror, in our selves as other selves.

In his discussion of *But We Are Exiles*, Russell Brown suggests that there is a parallel between Peter Guy's story and the myth of Narcissus ("Robert Kroetsch," *The Oxford Companion to Canadian Literature*). But the Lacanian "mirror image" suggests something more theoretically complex. Unlike Narcissus, Peter does not *just* fall in love with an image of himself; he is obsessed with the *mirror* images of two significant *others*—"this woman and what he thought was his best if very new friend" (48)—and of his own implication in that scene of otherness. Peter is caught and imaged with them. The mirror both exposes and hides, contains and distances, produces an image of the self and yet posits the self as other; it makes "identity . . . at once impossible and unavoidable" (Kroetsch, *Excerpts from the Real World*).

The fragmented, partial, incomplete nature of identity is mirrored in the structure of Peter's story. The book is divided, by white spaces in the text, into a series of parts differentiated by the use of italics. Interestingly, the italics themselves do not articulate any obvious differences. The first time the italics appear they begin mid-paragraph:

> Peter took Hornyak down into the engine-room from the galley *and Hornyak bent over a bin of tangled extension cords and loose bulbs and rolls of tape and pulled out a lamp that had no wire mask protecting the bulb.*

> *Peter hesitated, then said nothing.*
> *"Your old buddy," Hornyak said, "needs some light, Guy. What do you say?"*
> *Peter said nothing.*
> *"Guy you don't know your own mind. . . . My trouble is I know my own mind. And that's a terrible thing."* (9)

As this one does, many italicized sections contain material from the past. But much material from the past is not italicized. At the end of the novel, for instance, a narrative of Peter's past and the current narrative instant are juxtaposed with no change in the text's typographical presentation. Peter's *ex*/position in the present moment is suggested in the line, "He touched a hand to his eyes . . . he needed a glance in a mirror" (140). Moreover, this passage is followed immediately by a scene of dialogue between Mike Hornyak and Peter that took place six years ago. Peter is here and elsewhere. He has/is the alibi McAlpine says he will need (99). The alterations in tense and in typography destabilize the boundaries between present, past, and future, between significant and insignificant textual moments. There is no binary opposition or hierarchy of value established in the economy of either textual presentation of events or of narrative strategy. It is left to the reader to piece the pieces together, to "play" with the text and with the textualized figures represented there.

For example, like William William Dorfendorf in *Alibi*, Peter Guy is a comical and textually ambiguous "figure"—in the senses both of character and metaphor. Robert Wilson suggests that all of Kroetsch's characters are "examples of 'speaking names'"—the "character" is the name and that's all you need to know about her/him (*Labyrinths* 189). Kroetsch concurs, arguing that the name is a language act, it does not refer to a stable identity but indicates a role in the grammar of the story (190). Peter *is* a peter:

> "Be kind, Peter. Be Peter the Great."
> "At the rate I'm going, I'll be Peter the Pater."
> "Not at the rate you're going this morning."
> "I've got to go stand in the snow," he said.
> "Be Peter the Peter," she said, "Come back to bed."
> He watched her in the mirror. (76)

(The) Peter is a tease, a cheater, a delusion, a fraud, but nonetheless, amusing. In short, "Guy" likes to play with himself! "He" is not one.

Peter Guy literally plays at being a man. His name signifies both his stability (Peter is also the Rock) and his unpredictability ("the prick and its vagaries," Kroetsch, *Labyrinths*). Peter Guy signifies the emptiness of the phallic position, the lack at the centre of "male" authority. Like the figure of the woman, which, Kroetsch writes, is "silent at the center" of his writing (*Labyrinths* 22), Peter too is a present absence:

> *Peter hesitated, then said nothing.*
> *"Your old buddy," Hornyak said, "needs some light, Guy. What do you say?"*
> *Peter said nothing.*
> *"Guy, you don't know your own mind." . . . Sometimes I envy you. My trouble is I know my own mind. And that's a terrible thing. . . . I know till I want to wring one shout from that jesusly silent throat of yours."* (9)

Peter cannot give Hornyak some "light"; he has no faith in "understanding," in sending postcards with messages. Formerly, "running [was] the essence" (18), but Hornyak's death "gives it all another meaning. The running had long been a running away—from land, from people, from the confusion of loading and unloading, from checking the mail . . . a running away . . . from home" (19-20). The "home Peter had to go back to was a scattering of relatives" (59). Home is not a centre, but a scattering.

Unlike the lamp, the mirror offers an alibi, a complicity between love and writing: "he believed he did not want to believe what he saw, the eloquence of flesh and desire caught dispassionately in the glass mirror" (48). "The scene duplicates, repeats, and betrays itself," writes Derrida, "within the scene" (20). It is the spokenness, the "eloquence," of flesh and desire that betrays: Peter is betrayed not by flesh but by words; the mirror/language/eloquence tells (on) him.

But We Are Exiles both posits and undermines the sense (ex/posed as nonsense) of stable identity characteristic of realist fiction; it offers the "light" of story and yet the story is seen (scenes) in mirrors. Like Derrida's concept of erasure, in this early book Kroetsch unwittingly uses (the "light" of) realist conventions and then draws a tentative "X" through them (breaks the lamp). At the end of a detailed description of the daily routines on the riverboat, Kroetsch writes that it is "an order maintained as precariously as that maintained by the hands on the wheel. The chaos held in check . . ." (19). These words speak also for the form of the novel and for the literary theory Kroetsch is working within and out of at this point. Although *But We Are Exiles* seems to maintain the precarious order necessary to the "interpretation" of realist fiction, these conventions only hold the postmodernist chaos in precarious check. We can choose to affirm the free play of the text, or not. It is this desire to both stop the play and yet continue the game – a doubled desire not unlike the feminist impulse to both use and question the concept of woman – that indicates the feminist theory of subjectivity I find in so much of Robert Kroetsch's later work, to which I now turn.

CHAPTER FIVE

How *The Studhorse Man* Makes Love: Writing in a New Country

It is a grosse mistake in Architecture, to think that every small stud bears the main stresse and burthen of the building, which lies (indeed) upon the principal timbers.

—*Artificiall hansomenesse. A discourse of auxiliary beauty, or artificiall hansomenesse* 1656

In my eagerness to understand him completely [I] began on that particular occasion to take extensive notes on his past. Not trusting to memory, I borrowed paper and a pencil from the blind old lady who hovered constantly in the shadowy rooms beyond us. . . . Hazard was, I believe, flattered at the prospect of becoming a fictitious character. I at the time imagined I would write a wonderfully eloquent love story; indeed, anything but a biography.

—*The Studhorse Man*

Love is an affliction, and by the same token it is a word or a letter.

—Kristeva, *Tales of Love*

In different ways, each of my chapters has argued that feminist readers of Kroetsch's writing may find in it challenges to patriarchal authority, an "effing" of the "ineffable," a ridiculing of our attempts to fix a transcendental signified, a deferral of the possibility of word made flesh, a doubled space which de Lauretis signals as a(-)woman. Kroetsch plays "on the edge of convention," takes the risk of "falling right into language" and effects a kind of "erasure of self" (*Labyrinths* 50). To adopt a deconstructive lexis, Kroetsch's texts undermine Western philosophical discourse—the metaphysics of presence—which posits given and accessible meaning and identity ("what is popularly termed the 'real thing'" [*The Studhorse Man* 138]). In *The Studhorse Man*, the contradictory subject is problematized by a doubled sexual identity. Demeter/Hazard is a he/she who, in speaking, gestures toward the multiplication of meaning inherent in signification. A "stud" is both a "post" and "a stallion kept for breeding" (*The Oxford English Dictionary*). Like the"post (-man)," the "stud (-horse man)" is both fixed and disseminating. *The Studhorse Man* is not the studhorse man—as if the "truth of the man" could be in *either* the man or his biography (*The Studhorse Man* 134). *The Studhorse Man* is only "artificially" "him"-"self."

As in architecture, so too in writing/loving (Kroetsch: "without writing, I sometimes suspect, there would be no such thing as love"). And Demeter Proudfoot—(mad) biographer, (rival) lover, (he) she—finds it a "grosse mistake" to think that "every small stud bears the main stresse and burthen" of the narrative building: "If ever I complete my herculean study of that lonely man I shall call it not simply *Hazard Lepage: The Biography of a Modern Martyr, His Mortal Life and Immortal Accomplishments*, but rather, by devious means pointing to more significant dimensions, *The Stinting of Martha Proudfoot*" (142). In writing/loving, there are always more significant dimensions. "The" man is not at the centre. The studhorse man is, in the end, elsewhere; the lonely man (Hazard) is a woman (Martha). So how *does The Studhorse Man* make love?

Although it began as an "eloquent love story," Demeter Proudfoot's narrative of Hazard Lepage is an attempt to let Hazard be himself, to produce his biography. But what is the relation, the text asks, between subjectivity, writing, and loving, in a place where stable identity comes "by chance" (Hazard), by mistake, where the biography fails? Hazard Lepage can never be himself. His two names indicate a contradictory identity. Although Hazard is the "man" of the page, by the end of the text, "he" is also the narrator: "That morning I," says Demeter, "was D. Proudfoot, Studhorse Man" (156).

The figure of Demeter/Hazard signifies a slippage in sexual and textual identity. Neither and yet both "he" and "she," Demeter is a woman who is not one. "S/he" cannot be held in place. S/he is not a woman or a man. From the beginning, Demeter is, like the studhorse man, occupied with dissemination in a world that seeks to be "fixed" (in all senses—sterilized, put in order, made to work again). While

Hazard wants to breed "the perfect horse" (20), Demeter wants to breed with words. While he says he wants to capture Hazard in a biography, what he does is "take extensive notes on his past." "Whoever thought," asks Hazard Lepage, "that screwing would go out of style?" (11). For Demeter, the mad bathtub biographer, the style is the screwing. The question follows, "how do you make love in a new country?" "One way to make love is by writing," Kroetsch argues in "On Being an Alberta Writer"—an essay which also asks the analogous question, "how do you write in a new country?" (70-71). Jeanette Seim answers by saying that "Kroetsch creates a sexuality of textuality" (47). I argue rather that *The Studhorse Man* creates a textuality of sexuality. Although the title itself places *The Studhorse Man* outside the realm of what has traditionally been defined as "feminine" and although much of its content, if considered apart from its narrative strategies and procedures, seems to be "sexist," the textualization of not only sexuality but the whole, real world undermines the possibility of fixed or uncontradictory meaning.

Hélène Cixous describes feminine writing as texts which, like *The Studhorse Man*, "work on the difference." I suggest that feminine writing is also a way of reading which, according to Toril Moi, "struggle[s] to undermine the dominant phallogocentric logic, split[s] open the closure of the binary opposition and revel[s] in the pleasures of open-ended textuality" (*Sexual/Textual Politics* 108). This kind of feminist reading practice *is* writing in a new country.

Seim cites Kroetsch's sexualization of textuality in the following passage; I note the way Kroetsch's reading of textual politics overturns phallogocentric sexual assumptions:

> we conceive of external space as male, internal space as female. . . . The maleness verges on mere absence. The femaleness verges on mystery: it is a space that is not a space. External space is the silence that needs to speak, or that needs to be spoken. It is male. The having spoken is the book. It is female. It is closed. ("The Fear of Women in Prairie Fiction" 47)

Kroetsch posits the heretofore self-present male as "mere absence." His definition of the female is equally dislocating in terms of traditional categories. Not silent at all, the female is "the having spoken," "the book." But if "she" is like "the book," "she" too is both closed and open. Like the text itself "she" is infinitely misreadable, unfixable, plural. "How do you make love in a new country?" The pleasures of textuality and sexuality become interchangeable, and the possibilities of loving are the possibilities of writing. "In a paradoxical way, stories—more literally books—contain the answer" ("The Fear of Women" 47).

In the following scene, Hazard Lepage, studhorse man, seeks to describe the breasts of one P. Cockburn. The text self-consciously comments on the linguistic difficulties inherent in this effort. Although "the" P. Cockburn that Demeter locates *was* "single," Hazard "described her as a wealthy married women" (31). "Her" identity is repeatedly destabilized. Is she "single," or not? While Demeter's research located a "prominent religious family by the name of Cockburn," Hazard claimed "that her name was Coburne or Cochrane" (31). Nevertheless,

> This P. Cockburn, *he announced*, was a shade wrung in the withers, which *I take it meant* she was showing *signs* of her age and was therefore older than Martha. But, *he went on*, her tits were *like* nothing so much as two great speckled eggs of a rare wild bird. And *having said* this . . . *he fell to musing* about eggs of various birds, hoping to find a *comparison* that might be for me illuminating. (35; italics mine)

Does this passage fragment the female body through naming? Or does it also destabilize the supposedly stable, male, narrating self? "He" is undermined by his own speaking. "She" is a textual entity whose "signs" can only be misread.

Recall that the narrator in this passage and in the paragraphs that follow is *not* Hazard at all but Demeter—a "man" signified by a woman's name. All of the sexual encounters described in the book are Demeter's retellings of Hazard's narrative tellings. Try as the *reader* might, Demeter never forgets the writtenness of the book. Phrases like "(I prefer the archaic spelling)" (63) or "In a chapter that was seized by one of my doctors, I discuss at some length" (98), or "I too would like the preceding chapter to be more explicit" (144) insist that we recognize the narrative context of the narrative. Demeter is always telling (on) Hazard; Demeter, too, is a reader as well as a writer.

Demeter Proudfoot is adrift on a textual "sea": "I too get dressed up—by taking off my clothes. Sometimes of a morning I fold a three-by-five card into a little triangular hat and set it squarely on my perky fellow's noggin and pirates we sail here together in my bathtub, our cargo the leatherbound books and the yellow scribblers, the crumbling newspaper clippings and the envelopes with the cancelled stamps and the packs of note-cards that make up the booty of our daring'' (39). The power of the male pen(is), now a be-hatted "perky fellow," a "pirate," a fellow thief in reading, is ridiculed. A mad bathtub pirate takes the formerly privileged position of biographer, afloat, not with historical facts, but with "crumbling newspaper clippings," "leatherbound books," and "yellow scribblers." That the "I" of this passage is signified by the indeterminate signifier "Demeter"—a woman's name, mistakenly conferred upon a male body—is itself a deconstruction of what Terry Eagleton would speak of as the cocksure position of the phallogocentric self.

Without a privileged place from which to speak, without a privileged "I" (eye) with which to see, the power of the male gaze becomes impossible. "His" "I" sees only backward images in bathroom mirrors. Demeter can only reconstruct Hazard's re-presentation of a "woman" whose body re-presents herself—"she was showing signs of her age." "S/he" (Demeter? Hazard?) can proceed from metaphor to metaphor, from textual manoeuvre to textual manoeuvre ("he announced," "he went on," "having said," "he fell to musing") attempting to make the woman and her absent breast present. But to no end. There is no end to metaphor: "I confessed that I had never seen a chickadee's egg (though I have gone to some pains since in a vain attempt to find one)" (36). Demeter's interpretation ("I take it meant") repeatedly fails. Although Hazard continues to be "intent on refining still further his, shall we say, argument" (36), the more Hazard speaks the less Demeter understands. All s/he can tell is difference.

Passages of this kind (and there are others) suggest that in speaking one always says more, other, and differently than "one" means; meaning and identity ("I was priest to his long confession" [36]) are not only implicated but duplicated in the "telling." A later reference to a male lover ("Stiff") telling his beloved (named, what else, "Hole"), "your breasts . . . are like the great speckled—" (56) suggests again that this text mimics male conventions which make a fetish of women's body parts and insists instead that the more dangerous fetish is metaphor: "is it not / a commonplace, for instance, to compare the undulating / hills of whatever distant horizon to the breasts of a / nearby woman, or vice versa" ("The Sad Phoenician" 86).

Given the attention to metaphor—to dissemination—in this text, it comes as no surprise that subjectivity is differentially (and deferentially) defined. The studhorse man is both (and neither) Demeter and Hazard and the book itself. As Hazard says to his alter ego "'Demeter? Is that you?' 'No,' I shouted back mocking him. 'No. I am the man who breeds horses. Who are you?' . . . 'I'm with you'" (161). *The Studhorse Man* is both the studhorse man and the stud/horseman: "the cry half horse, half man, the horse-man cry of pain or delight" (169). "He" is caught (textualized) "horsing" around:

> I could not see clearly in that faint light, but a tall thin (it looked like wax) statue of something or other reflected the candle's glow and I am certain of what I saw. They were both of them, Hazard and Marie, on the far side of the high old bed—they were both down on their hands and knees. . . .
>
> "Hazard?" I whispered, not daring to think or consider.
>
> I swear before God and man that he whinnied. (133)

In "The Fear of Women in Prairie Fiction" Kroetsch speaks of the horse/house binary opposition—what Seim calls the "basic grammatical pair in the story line of prairie fiction" (47). *The Studhorse Man* undermines that binary: "this nut here . . . keeps horses in his house" (14). Moreover, unlike the traditional male, Hazard is "homesick" (70): "he felt secure in his old house; it was the road he dreaded, travel" (11).

Like the dramatic undermining of the house/horse distinction, the male/female binary opposition, too, is destabilized. Of what sexual identity is Demeter Proudfoot? He? She? It is impossible to *tell.* As Kroetsch writes of *As For Me and My House* and *My Antonia*, "We cannot even discover who is protagonist. . . . Male or female? . . . Horse or house?" ("The Fear of Women" 55). Once the categories of both male/female and the self are undermined it becomes equally impossible to say that "one" is (only) subject or object, one looking, another looked at, one on the horse, another in the house—we are both one and the other. To name the "man" narrating *The Studhorse Man* is to name a woman: Demeter.

Consider again the failed disseminator Hazard Lepage. Like Demeter, who is always searching for and wondering/wandering over the "proper name" ("The mind wanders. What a strange expression" [135]), Hazard too has a "certain flourish with names" (72). "In the act of naming we distinguish ourselves from the other unfortunate animals with whom we share this planet," Demeter writes, "They seem under no necessity to deny the fact that we are all, so to speak, one—that each of us is, possibly, everyone else" (119). In other words, the self is always already elsewhere; when I say "I" I speak an/other's name. "The" studhorse man—Hazard Lepage/Demeter Proudfoot—is and is not both male and female, writer and reader, absent and present. Shirley Neuman:

> The telling of a particular myth in a Kroetsch novel then must be analogous to the act of deconstructing myth itself. It would not be unlike the turning of a particular myth, say the quest myth, into the activity of the writer: the activity of Demeter, rather than the activity of Hazard Lepage. (*Labyrinths* 96)

But the activity of Demeter as writer is also the activity of Demeter as woman—both literally, "Forgive my misfortune—my dear mother, pretending knowledge and believing Demeter to be a masculine name, affixed it to my birth certificate" (64)—and politically—as Luce Irigaray writes, "'She' is indefinitely other in herself. That is undoubtedly the reason she is called temperamental, incomprehensible, perturbed, capricious—not to mention her language in which 'she' goes off in all directions and in which 'he' is unable to discern the coherence of any meaning" (103).

Like the French feminist figure of woman as that which exists outside the symbolic order, Demeter/Hazard is a trickster, "he's very subversive, very carnivalesque." Furthermore, Kroetsch writes, "the trickster is often tricked. That intrigues me. I suppose there is a kind of sexual origin in the figure of the trickster—the prick and its vagaries—but at the same time this instills a sense of the absurdity of all sexuality" (*Labyrinths* 100). Like the writer as woman the trickster has an irrational, immoral impulse. There is "no logic to his system, only anti-logic" (*Labyrinths* 99). Her/his play is in and of words.

Phallogocentrism depends on the unchanging meaning of the phallus, a word upon which *The Studhorse Man* wages many a linguistic battle:

> "You tool," Hazard said. "You faltering apparatus."
> "You whang and rod and pud," the trucker replied.
> "You drippy dong. You Johnny and jock." (43)

Nonetheless, the "meaning" of "Old Blue," the "core of Hazard's being" (42), depends entirely on difference: "you diddly dink. You d-you d- you dink. You dick" (43). To attempt to fix meaning is to hesitate, to stutter. Even Hazard's death warning is a play on words: "*La mer sera votre meurtrière*" (12). The phrase plays on the words "mer" (as mother, sea, see, horse, whore's) but it is the letter that both kills and re/places him: Demeter (named by "chance"/Hazard?) assumes "his" subject position. "The" "mer" is (merely? mirrorly?) plural. Even the "horse" is a "mare," present in/as both writing and loving: "He variously shortened the true name to Posse or Poesy or Pussy" (11).

Demeter is the mad(wo)man—"I am by profession quite out of my mind" (61). S/he is reconstructing images ("seaing" what s/he can see, horsing around, mirrorly playing?): "a mirror is so placed above my sink that I have been able to sit for hours, attempting to imagine what in fact did happen (allowing for the reversal of the image) exactly where I imagine it" (85). S/he is writer/hero/reader/storyteller/deconstructor; the one who speaks, and is spoken by, the book. S/he is finally, like Anna Dawe, the "daughter" who calls herself by a textual name that is not her father's: "D. Lepage, she now calls herself; and she has grown up to be something of a lover of the horse" (174).

"In the end," so to speak, the names Demeter Proudfoot and Hazard Lepage come together in the figure of Demeter Lepage: bastard daughter of speech—her father is Eugene "Utter"—"a windbag from beginning to end" (86). Demeter Lepage figures feminine writing. *The Studhorse Man*, "this portentous volume" (portentous: "like a portent": "omen, significant sign of something to come"—always already disseminating) is, in the endless end, dedicated to her. The other Demeter asked, "Why is the truth never where it should be? Is the truth of the man in the man or in his biography? Is the truth of the beast in the flesh and confusion or in the few skillfully arranged lines?" (134). Well, yes, and no. With the writing of Derrida and Cixous *The Studhorse Man* speaks as a difference within itself, at the deconstruction of binary oppositions (like *either* the man *or* his biography) finds the truth in the fiction. The studhorse man is a woman.

The Studhorse Man takes the methods of deconstruction in order to undermine those categories (even the category of category) which make singular identity possible. It offers a site on which there is no privileged position from which to speak and suggests that when we write we are always in a new country. Moreover, the text insists on the writtenness and instability of sexual identity. We are each, like Demeter the biographer, readers and writers: "the biographer must naturally record, he must also be interpretative upon occasion" (28). As readers we play with *The Studhorse Man* (as Peter Guy does in *But We Are Exiles*, to be/guile it), let slip the notion of sexual identity, and partake in the endlessness of textuality and sexuality figured in Hazard/Demeter/D. Lepage.

Like much contemporary deconstructive theory, *The Studhorse Man* worries over the end of dissemination, the imposition of order in a chaotic world, the desire for simplicity in the face of complexity—the issue that speech and writing see "I" to "I" on:

> Scurrilous, barbarous, stinking man would soon be able, in the sterility of his own lust, to screw himself into oblivion, to erase himself like a rotting pestilence from the face of God's creation: Utter and I surely saw eye to eye on that issue. (174)

Sexual desire, procreation, and birth control become metaphors for textual play, dissemination, and the fixing of meaning. Homologically, the "pill" arrests the pregnancy of signification and sterilizes language. It is not in the sterilizing but in the "teazing" (in both the sexual and textual senses noted on page 63 of *The Studhorse Man*) out of the possibilities of meanings and of multiple sexual subject positions, that *The Studhorse Man*'s gesture toward the future of human sexual/textual relations lies.

CHAPTER SIX

"This Version of Man": Telling the Story with *What the Crow Said*

Kroetsch, the master story-teller *in print*, an A-1 Hard Northern bullshitter who nevertheless doesn't "tell" stories except when he writes them down (so he tells us), doesn't so much tell the stories of the people and parties he encounters along the way as he alludes to them.

—Barbour

People, years later, blamed everything on the bees; it was the bees, they said, seducing Vera Lang, that started everything. How the town came to prosper, and then to decline, and how the road never got built, the highway that would have joined the town and the municipality to the world beyond, and how the sky itself, finally, took umbrage: it was all because one afternoon in April the swarming bees found Vera Lang asleep, there in a patch of wild flowers on the edge of the valley.

—*What the Crow Said*

Examine carefully the behaviour of these people:
Find it surprising though not unusual
Inexplicable though normal
Incomprehensible though it is the rule.
Consider even the most insignificant, seemingly simple,
Actions with distrust. Ask yourselves whether it is necessary.
Especially if it is usual.
We ask you expressly to discover
That what happens all the time is not natural.
For to say that something is natural
In such times of bloody confusion
Of ordained disorder, of systematic arbitrariness
Of inhuman inhumanity is to
Regard it as unchangeable.

—Brecht, *The Exception and the Rule*

If the "natural"—the behaviour of people, simple actions, what happens all the time—is the subject of the classic realist text, the subject of *What the Crow Said* is the *unnatural.* After all, the world of the text is one in which bees seduce and impregnate women, futures are remembered, crows speak, summer never comes. The world of the text *is* a world *of* text, of reports, gossip, tall-tales, bullshit. As Brecht does, *What the Crow Said* asks us to reread the "natural" to see that that which is incomprehensible does not have to be the rule. In *What the Crow Said* the "bloody confusion" is welcome because it is textual confusion, made to be misread.

Gertrude Stein's "A Sound" offers the kind of paradoxically recognizable and yet meaningless world we find in *What the Crow Said*: "Elephant beaten with candy and little pops and chews all bolts and reckless reckless rats, this is this" (*Tender Buttons* 474). Jon Erickson notes that "the potency of this imaging relies on its tension with the conventional system of meaning (as does Magritte's painting of a pipe, *Ceci n'est pas une pipe*) rather than on a discarding of that system for a new one" (279). In *What the Crow Said* there is a similar invocation of the conventional system of meaning and an insistence on the misrecognition of alternatives. In *What the Crow Said*, as in Stein's and Magritte's work, "the meaning never really surfaces." According to Erickson: "the delineation of its dim signifying form, refracted by the surface words, rests most fully on the projective ability of the interlocutor" (279).

Like Liebhaber, we too are "desperately trying to make sense of those absurd acts . . . flying in the air and so on" (Kroetsch, *Labyrinths* 163). In Kroetsch's words, it is the "sense of active reading, of being an active reader" (*Labyrinths* 162) that tells (the) story. The reader works at and plays in the text because the possibility of interpretation—and of the interpretation of interpretation—is, as it is in the following journal entry, repeatedly offered and resisted: "Trying to begin again I invent my theory of the uninvention of the world, then plot anew . . . beginning to see what is not quite. The farther shaping against the central notes. How to circumference the moving point" (*The "Crow" Journals* 12). To shift the metaphor, *What the Crow Said* is an archaeology of knowledge. Edward Said argues that Foucault looks at "knowledge whose practice conceals its own fabrication" ("An Ethics of Language" 32). As I noted in Chapter Three,

Kroetsch is, like Foucault, interested in archaeology as a metaphor for the reading process. Kroetsch's work often makes modes of production of textual knowledge apparent, foregrounds the processes by which a knowledge is made to seem "natural." Against the assertions of the classic realist text, Kroetsch's story is meta-story, a tale of itself.

Traditionally, the classic realist text has been read as offering a position of knowledge to the reader. Although events and characters are *always made* to *seem* present, the classic realist text conceals the process of production, effaces the fabrication which makes (re)presentation possible. What Catherine Belsey calls the "interrogative text" works instead by interrogating its own procedures. The interrogative text

> disrupts the unity of the reader by discouraging identification with a unified subject of enunciation. The position of the "author" inscribed in the text, if it can be located at all, is seen as questioning or as literally contradictory . . . it literally invites the reader to produce answers to the questions it implicitly or explicitly raises. (*Critical Practice* 91)

Interrogatively, Kroetsch's texts undertake an archaeology of their own knowledges. They speak of their own processes of production and in so speaking question themselves.

The following passage indicates the kind of interrogation of its own knowledges—here it appears in the form of a deferral to other texts—that goes on in *What the Crow Said*:

> The black crow, *according to all reports*, flew away, flew south, that very day. It had recently taken to napping a lot, expecially [*sic*] after meals. *Some people claimed* that as it left it called out, one last time, "Total asshole." *Most people argued* that it left without *saying a word*; it flapped up into the sky; it flew, tossed and torn and ragged, *the way any crow flies*, into the wild shuffling of the everlasting wind. (148; italics mine)

What the Crow Said offers, not finished, coherent, unified story—the text does not simply tell us that the black crow flew south—but traces of unfinished, indeed unfinishable, text—the text tells more than it can say: "according to all *reports*" the crow flew "the way any crow flies." Kroetsch says, of *What the Crow Said*, "sometimes I would throw away what another novelist would make seventy pages or a novel out of. There are fragments out of which the reader can almost make up a novel" (*Labyrinths* 14). "Almost" is the telling word in this phrase: we *have* only text—"reports" and "arguments."

In *What the Crow Said* Kroetsch offers, not specific, consumptive knowledge (a story) but a process of production, a way of treating—or retreating from—story, a game:

> It's interesting that we play the game, isn't it. There is a double thing that goes on even in the statement which is very fascinating to me. The two words contradict each other in a signifying way. *Play* resists the necessary rules of the *game*. (*Labyrinths* 50)

Kroetsch is fascinated with the "double thing" that goes on, with telling as difference, with words that contradict each other. Just as play resists the necessary rules of the game, so does telling resist the necessary rules of story. To tell is not to tell, and it is also to tell otherwise.

William Gass's "in the heart of the heart of the country" celebrates story as telling in this sense:

> A Place
> SO I HAVE sailed the seas [c's? sees?] and come . . .
> to B [be? bee?] . . .
> a small town fastened to a field in Indiana.
> (Stevick 132)

Kroetsch writes, in *The "Crow" Journals*, "Last night, read again William Gass's *In the Heart of the Heart of the Country*" [*sic*] (26). *What the Crow Said* begins: "People, years later, blamed everything on the bees" (7). "I go on reading about bees" Kroetsch writes, "the newest temptation: to become, against all this, a beekeeper. . . . But then the bees, so quickly, would make me one of their workers, a part of their design and intent" (*The "Crow" Journals* 69). To b/be/bee or not to b/be/bee, these are the questions.

Although Kroetsch says he "didn't yet know her name," the writing of Vera Lang began in the Qu'Appelle Valley Saskatchewan: "watching a young woman who was also sitting in the sun writing. . . . That woman, writing her story, unwittingly writing mine" (*The "Crow" Journals* 22). Vera Lang is a woman seduced by "b/e/es"—she is a writer—"it was the bees, they said, seducing Vera Lang, that started everything. . . . It was all because one afternoon in

April the swarming bees found Vera Lang asleep" (7). Like Kroetsch, "she" is a "beekeeper"—"their total involvement in the mystery . . . stories, always, of swarming" (*The "Crow" Journals*). Vera Lang "herself, swarmed into a new being" (10) and emerged: "arrogantly pregnant, concentrating on her new books on bees, she prepared for the season of honey that she was certain must come" (37). Vera—the name paradigmatically linked to "verity," to truth—seduced by "swarming" b's—a disseminating "Lang"/language. Vera's name is itself a contradiction: it is "la langue" which makes a final "verity" impossible. The name itself (never itself) invoking the possibility and impossibility of signification; narrative as truth-telling (the "abc's," we could say) and as what a "bee" sees in a woman: the "meaning that doesn't quite mean," as Kroetsch writes in *The "Crow" Journals* (69).

The title of Kroetsch's book on b's (*What the Crow Said*) undermines the authority both of a "master storyteller"—the narrative *is* what the crow said—and of the narrating voice in the text which does not belong to a single speaker: "when I was writing *What the Crow Said*, beginning *Years later* . . . , suddenly just with that phrase, I had available to me all that people said years later, that whole fabric of gossip and story" (*Labyrinths* 169). The words "years later" suggest both legendary authority (you *can* tell years later) and the impossibility of the record (you *never* can tell). *What the Crow Said* is a text of gossip. If "people, years later, blamed everything on the bees," everything can be blamed, for example, on language—b-ing—or on the Heideggerian *dasein* of thrown-ness of existence—being (cf. *The "Crow" Journals* 23).

In *The "Crow" Journals* Kroetsch considers whether it is "language itself" which is the trickster (25). The "b-ing" of language, the "systematic arbitrariness," as Brecht might have said, is foregrounded in the figure of Liebhaber—"itinerant prairie printer, as center, as ultimate story center/teller" puts together a "mythic/epic/comic telltale of the family/town/ west of this version of man" (*The "Crow" Journals* 11): "He spent the afternoon of Tiddy's wedding day in his flat above the newspaper office, studying his collection of wood type, puzzling with his ink-stained fingers the intricate knot of language that bound him to death" (54-55). As teller "he" is decentred in "his" telling. As telltale, "this version of man" is a text, a gossip. "He" could be a woman.

Liebhaber tries to turn the "W" into an "M"—turning "water" to "mater." It is not the signified that concerns him. Liebhaber is, the narrator tells us, "in terror at the domestication of those free, beautiful letters—no, it was the absurdity of their recited order that afflicted him: ABCDEFGHIJKLMNOPQRSTUVWXYZ—he opened a twenty-six of rye and, with immense effort, tried to disentangle himself from the tyranny of rote" (69). In the end, "he" is "making sounds for which he had no signs at all" (69). For Liebhaber, it is the letter as wood piece that signifies.

Rita, like her sister Vera Lang, is a writer. Her perpetual play with letters addresses the question of the writer's relation to language and desire. The name "Rita" itself is a pun on the words "writer" and "reader." Rita is only a writer, however (*she* is a post-man!), who never reads the letters she therefore *doesn't* "receive":

> She wrote erotic letters to those imprisoned men, spoke of her longing, of her dream. . . . She caressed their thighs with words. . . . She had no other admirers, no lovers, only those men whose names she found in the newspapers. And she never opened the letters she received. (88)

Liebhaber, the "lover" (of words), "hated her for those unread letters, those secret, unopened letters. They tempted him to imagine what desperate pleadings they might contain, what longing, what despair" (88).

Both "JG" and "Vera's boy" figure the relation between language, silence, and meaning played with in *Crow*. John Gustav—son of both, and so neither, Skandl and Liebhaber—lacks speech, "expresses" himself by filling his pants (79). "Whether or not the crow was speaking what was on the silent child's mind, that was never clearly determined. But there were those who insisted that the black crow sometimes spoke on behalf of JG" (64). But the crow is, variously a "prick with ears" *and* a woman:

> They asked what she had said to silence the black crow.
>
> "*Schwarzkopf*," Art Van Slyke said. "All she said to the crow was *Schwarzkopf*."
>
> "She's no fool," Liebhaber said. He was surprised to hear himself defending the black crow. But he couldn't stop himself: "She told me . . ."

> "*She*?" Andy Wolbeck interrupted. "What the hell do you mean, *she*? What is this *she* stuff?" (97)

The crow offers both phallic power (speech, the prick) and undermines that power—the crow, too, is a woman.

While what the crow says is being silenced, Vera's boy "jabbers on, hardly stopping to listen, in a kind of speech that was half yips and barks, half what his listeners took to be pig latin" (135). Vera's boy has been raised by coyotes—trickster figures in Kroetsch's work, figures for language itself. The boy's talent for reading signs, for predicting the weather, is undermined by the one "only and minor"—significant, in terms of the possibilities of meaning—difficulty that when he spoke it was a "language that no one quite understood" (139). The one who *could* read the "signs" could not be understood. His readings were unreadable.

The crow, signified speaker of the novel, is more articulate than either JG or Vera's boy. But the crow arrives late, leaves early in the narrative, disappears when JG dies: "the black crow, according to all reports, flew south, that very day" (148) and most people argued that "to all reports"—and who can trust them?—it "left without saying a word" (148). Like the crow, much of the narrative leaves without *saying* a word; it is the *writing* that tells all. *What the Crow Said* is, and is not, what the crow said!

Like the crow, story and character are absent presences. Robert Lecker sees "all of the characters who populate *Crow*" as "metafictional constructs" (100). The reader is left to reconstruct the links between what we are told has happened and how we suppose the "effect" was caused. For example, how *does* Anna Marie become pregnant?

> A young man from a neighboring farm, Nick Droniuk, was hired to help out with the herd while Liebhaber was absent. One day, watching a teazer cow excite a bull, he became so excited that he accidentally inserted himself in the semen-collecting device. Anna Marie, Tiddy's third daughter was assigned to mix the semen with egg yolk, then to measure it off into quantified units for insertion, with a pipette, into various brands of cow. . . . Hardly two months after Nick's initial experiment, Anna Marie made her announcement. (71)

Like the archaeologist, we are left with artifacts (artful facts? Anna Marie is pregnant), but we must invent the narrative (we can imagine what Anna must have done with one of those pipettes). As Kroetsch says, the "temptation of meaning is upon us all the time" (*Labyrinths* 14). Rather than "story," perhaps "saying" better describes *What the Crow Said*—the temptation of meaning is a narrative device; the pieces of story are given to tempt us into the game of reading, into putting together meaning, *telling* the story.

The "play" (of *différance*) that goes on in a game, says Kroetsch, is precisely that which resists the rules (*Labyrinths* 49). For the reader to "play" the reading game in *What the Crow Said* s/he can transgress the rules as much as the writer does, putting together *or* dismantling the text in whatever way s/he chooses, telling her story. Consider, for example, the opening of Chapter Ten: "The wedding was held on a cold morning just a few days after Easter Sunday, in the Church of the Final Virgin. Why Tiddy Lang chose John Skandl out of all her 24 suitors was never explained to anyone's satisfaction" (51). The impossibility of knowing or "telling" or explaining to anyone's satisfaction what the crow said, the truth of the story, is, as it is here, a subject of the story and of any reading of the story.

The arrival of the bees in Chapter One is a metaphor for the play of difference which goes on in the game, for the telling of difference as story: "the bees, streaming, shaped into a streamer of brown and gold, high in the sparkle of sun, began to drift toward the place where Vera waited. . . . For how long she lay transfixed there was never a way to *tell*" (9; italics mine). At once multiple ("bees, streaming") and singular ("a [phallic] streamer"), like the speaking subject, the bees vacillate between sexual subject positions, between the singleness of phallic authority and the multiplicity of erotic pleasuring: there is never a way to tell.

In the end, who knows *What the Crow Said*? What should have been the crow's words—"caw caw caw caw caw"—are repeatedly said by the men—"a bunch of useless bastards" (88; 14). It is the telling that matters. Moreover, it sounds like the men are saying "cock cock cock cock cock." You never can tell. When the crow reappears near the end of the text s/he is "talking, not listening, croaking endlessly on"; but "Liebhaber cannot quite understand what the crow is saying. . . . Perhaps it is talking through the window"

(217). Perhaps the crow *is* talking "through the window," with the conventions of the classic realist text which is based on seeing through windows. But like Liebhaber, we cannot quite understand what the crow said.

"Perhaps," the text interprets itself, the crow is "telling Liebhaber that morning has come." But Liebhaber doesn't speak out loud "for fear of waking Tiddy." Neither does the narrator "speak." The absent narrator is the voice of the community who "tells" us by not supposing the story can be told. This is a narrative that says "People, years later, blamed everything on the bees," but leaves the story open to interpretation. The text ends with Cathy—named, significantly, in light of my opening argument, "the normal one"—walking across the pasture:

> Sometimes she stops to look at a crocus, wet and closed. The crows are cawing. Sometimes she stops. . . . Sometimes she does not wonder at all, sometimes she talks to herself, sometimes she looks at the sky, hoping that Joe Lightning will fall into her arms. (218)

There is a sense in which the "natural" has been restored. "Crows are cawing." "She" is normal. Like the page and a half prior to the ending, in this paragraph we are no longer hearing a narrative that is told "years later." We are in a present when "It is morning." But it is a present that is more like a Liebhaberian "remembered future." The repetition of the word "sometimes" calls the entire narrative into question. Like the word "perhaps," "sometimes" suggests that these are repeated, though not necessary, gestures—"There was never a way to tell" (9)—there is no way of knowing or telling the moment "as"—in the senses of both "at the moment when" and "the way in which"—that ever dubious "it" occurs. The best the narrator, indeed narration, can "tell" is that "sometimes" these things happen.

What the Crow Said is a book of traces, a collection of sayings, a narrative of absence, which can be made to represent, metonymically, the (w)hole from which they have come. The "story" can be read as "telling" that which it does not presume to know; it is simply, and enigmatically, "what the crow said." Like the archaeologist, we gather our fragments and speculate on the events that might "sometimes" have occurred, be(e)cause . . . we narrate our own "sayings." But, you never can tell. Like the archaeologist's, our stories are only "speculations." In a sense we speak from mirrors (we do not look through windows) in doubled seeings/sayings that are always betraying themselves, telling the difference. After Brecht, *What the Crow Said* teaches us that all our see(m)ing knowledges are merely speculations that invite us to reread stories of the past into changeable presents (texts *are* gifts), and futures.

CHAPTER SEVEN

Alibis for Being(,) Lost

In this chapter, I am especially concerned, not with our ability to act within certain prescribed sexual roles, but with how these roles circumscribe what we are. Kroetsch's work, like much postmodernist fiction, art, and poetry, moves us into what Greg Ulmer speaks of as a "post-age" in which "one" can be a male subject – be "maled," so to speak – only by assuming an alibi. Jamal points out that the word "alibi" signifies both "elsewhere" and a "plea that when an alleged act took place one was elsewhere" (5). To assume an alibi – and to acknowledge that in speaking we are always assuming alibis – is to acknowledge that our positions as sexual subjects are always already *ex*/positions – only provisionally granted, or held. William William Dorfendorf in *Alibi: A Novel* figures the displaced, ex/posed subject who speaks with an alibi: "sitting here. . . . I beg your pardon, there" (195). Like one of "his" lovers Manny, "she, he, that man or woman" (183), speaks – "I was telling myself the story" (26). But the story that "he" tells is (un)like "him"self, lost and found in the telling. "He" speaks, not as a unified, male-gendered subject, but as an alibi for being (lost).

Rather than focus on the ways the concept of a unified gendered subjectivity is undermined, I will, instead, locate the ways that the multiple texts of *Alibi* simultaneously undermine male position – singularity of voice, identity, sexual identity – and the strategies of telling – coherence, linearity, objectivity – peculiar to male expositions, because *Alibi* tells only differences within the stories it tells and the speakers it inscribes. Like Dorf, the "novel" *Alibi* insistently and repeatedly speaks of itself as precarious, absent from itself, multiple: "Yes, today, even while I tear out sheets from the front of the journal I write new notes on the sheets at the end" (230). The speaking subject, William William Dorfendorf, tells of his difference from himself:

> I'd had two grandfathers by the first name of William, both with the same first name, and my parents, farming people northeast of Calgary in the Battle River country, in a futile hope that I might receive at least one inheritance, named me after both of them. Billy Billy Dorfen. And all I got from my ancestors, it turned out, was the conviction that I needed two of everything: two cars, two university degrees, two bank accounts, two addresses, two mailboxes. For sure, two kicks at the cat. Two lives, possibly. (13)

The story is not "his" own; it "had no doubt been dictated by Jack Deemer himself" (195). The "self" of Jack Deemer is, as all written selves, the selves of all writers of messages are, "simply a name. And a legend of course" (13). Dorf has "never met Jack Deemer, at least not face to face; he's a great one for sending messages" (7). Like Dorf, Deemer's "minions live in a kind of dread of memos or post cards or, for that matter, scraps of toilet paper scrawled with instructions for which there is no explanation, no place to seek clarification" (7).

Alibi is an open letter, a post card sent without explanation; there is no return address. It is a "correspondence" that, as Derrida writes, immediately gets beyond us (*The Post Card* 7). The narrator's quest for the spa is based on misreadings which lead only to other writings: "Find me a spa, Dorf. That was the message. Nothing more, nothing less. Out of nowhere. For no reason. . . . Absurdly I turned the piece of paper upside down and tried to read it that way. . . . I wasn't quite sure what the hell a spa was" (7). Dorf's search for the "proper" interpretation (the perfect spa) is a search which leads only to other interpretations (other spas). Dorf's interrogation of the messages, his questioning of the writings, continues throughout the text in his further interpretations of the messages he receives, in his rereadings and rewritings of the journal entries, and in our own interrogations of the text(s) we are confronted with. By the end of the "novel" we are ready to ask, with Dorf, "what the hell isn't a message in this world we live in? And what is?" (199).

William William Dorfendorf, narrator, journal writer, I/I—"the" one who speaks as he is spoken—"acts out the collector's desire. The desire is his" (153). If, as Lecker argues, Dorf's boss Jack Deemer figures the author, now dead, "Dorf is an anagram for 'fraud,' for fiction" (112). Dorf is also a text: "I am the comic imitator of what he proposes in earnest" (*Alibi* 108). Dorfendorf (Dorf *and* Dorf?) makes and unmakes "him"-self (selves?) and "his" texts by rereading and rewriting: "The collection itself only confirms the discontinuity of this scattered world; it's my talk that puts it together. I rave the world into coherence for Deemer" (195). Yet for all his ravings and writings, the discontinuity, scatter, and incoherence which constitute the text, and the textualized self, of William William Dorfendorf, remains. He is no "re"-Deemer. Beginnings and endings are confused (a favourite preoccupation in Kroetsch's work) and Dorf—as reader and writer—is left, as we all are, to collect the fragments of the textual events: that collection is the story, the alibi, the multivocal self.

If the theory of narrative texts and the narratological manoeuvre describes how a narrative text produces meanings, how does *Alibi* "mean?" Dorf's "story"—in its illogicalities, fragmentations, and contradictions (*he* called it a manual of health)—undermines our attempts to describe "it" (as though it were one) within traditional narratological categories like *histoire*, *récit*, and *narration*. The "events" which constitute the story are continually deferred to and by further writings—messages, chapter titles, rewritings. There is no pretextual chronological order. The text is "out of order" in every possible sense: it does not work; it makes us work. Considering the novel as alibi makes a single or legitimate order impossible. There are no "events" apart from texts that account for them. The narrator is a textual construct, as vulnerable as the pages on which s/he is written. There is no single narrative text we could describe as originary, as, in any simple sense, "there." *Alibi*'s name is not its name; Dorf's transcription is not complete; some of the text is still called "Dorfendorf's Journal." While Dorf is on a quest for the perfect spa we are on our own impossible quests for the perfect text. Like Dorf, we find ourselves elsewhere.

Even the chapter titles offer a challenge to both the assumptions of narratology and of logocentrism. They do not summarize or explain the chapters which follow but offer both a lengthy narrative and a theory of narrative. In an untranscribed (or so we are told) journal entry Dorf writes, "let Karen put in some headings, some chapter titles to trap the unwary eye and lure the customer; she with her gift for compromise" (231). Is it Karen who, in terms of the narrative, calls *Dorfendorf's Journal* (as Dorf describes his "manual of health" [231]) (an?) *Alibi*? As alter-na(rra)tive, the chapter headings are spoken by a third person who refers to the struggling and decentred William William Dorfendorf as the unified "Dorf." But these headings also criticize and undermine the narrative, they do not stabilize it. "(OR, IN WHICH DORF CLAIMS TO HAVE GOT LAID)" signifies a story Dorf is not telling, but which nonetheless gets itself told. Story and text are not confined by notions of author and reader. We are all texts, and readers, as we write the narrative: "It's a plotted world we live in" (97).

What we might better speak of as the chapter "be/headings" are an unpredictable mixture of unfinished descriptions, warnings, and what Dorf calls "negatives." Like the ostensibly more accurate entries from "Dorfendorf's Journal" which end the work, the chapter headings impose a kind of sense on the reading experience we are having. Indeed, not only Dorf as journal writer but also Dorf as reader is "trying to make sense" of the journal, since the other "he" who told the other set of events (for the events change in rewritings) was "sometimes remiss, sometimes left little gaps here and there" (231).

Even if "Dorf" has made corrections where necessary, we have no way of knowing what the so-called "original entry" was—what the truth was. As Dorf's sister Sylvia—who "regarded herself as the guardian of truth and language, as if there was, somehow, a connection between the two"—points out, Dorf refuses "to tell the truth" (86). Dorf tells us that the "original notes, Karen's birthday journal to me, are only the negatives which now I develop" (232). Rather, it is the reader who is left with the negatives, the black marks, and if a story develops it is because of our "making do," as the message on Karen Strike's T-shirt says (22). We *make* the marks *do* something:

> "In my slight exaggerations," I said, "in my careful and deliberate tilting of the mirror, you might, if you chose to look, recognize truths that have forever been denied you."
>
> That was a little more than Sylvia could take.
>
> "A lie is a lie," she said, resorting to a tautology as moralists are wont to do. (86)

More self-consciously than the other chapters, "Negative #1: And Breakfast, After" and "Negative #2: Footloose: On Crutches" suggest they are untranscribed journal entries, existing as they had existed in the birthday journal. But the manuscript Dorf thinks he is finishing he calls a manual of health. What we find between the covers of this book is a jumble of postmodern verbiage. How do we use categories like story, text, or narration in such an anti-narrative?

The self-reflexive criticism of earlier printed versions of the novel that exists as part of the narrative text further problematizes the question. Passages of this kind suggest that there was no revision from journal to finished narrative. For example, the narrative describes Karen flipping open the "journal" to an entry we have just read in the "novel" (see how difficult it is to describe intra- and extra-textual writings?):

> "It says here that you 'didn't want to spoil Karen's response. Her pleasure.' "
>
> "That's absolutely correct" I said.
>
> "But you don't explain to either of us how a grown man happened to scald his prick . . . just at the moment when he might have done a little pleasuring." (61)

This scene argues that there is a difference between Dorf's perceptions of the earlier scene and Karen's interpretation, not only of the earlier scene, but also of Dorf's narrative account of the events that she experienced differently. Not insignificantly, it was a trusting of the relation between signifier and signified—the hot and cold water taps were misnamed ("assuming I could *tell* hot from cold" [121; italics added])—that began both the written event and the written critique of the written event.

Self-consciousness and self-reflexiveness about language and the processes of writing are central to the project of deconstruction and to the destabilization of patriarchal privilege. *Alibi* bullies readers into recognizing both its own narrative processes and our interpretive procedures as it carries out an almost carnivalesque deconstructive gymnastics. There is the text that we have in our hands called *Alibi: A Novel* that includes lengthy chapter headings and a section called "Dorfendorf's Journal." There is the text that Dorf writes he is writing as he is writing it—the journal that Karen gave him for his birthday. There is the text that Dorf is transcribing from journal entries into a text called *Dorfendorf's Journal: A Manual of Health*. There is the story of the events that happened to Dorf and Karen, to Dorf and Julie, to Dorf and Julie and Manny, to Dorf and Julie and Karen, and so on. There is the written story of the writing of these events. There is the written story of the rewriting of these events. But all of these textualized events are incomplete and told after the fact with errors and omissions. Where or what are *the* events of the narrative?

The multiplicitous nature of *Alibi* makes the Derridean point that all we have available to us are texts; alibis are always written. We know where we are and where we have been by our own inscriptions.

The paradoxical self-consciousness and self-denial of this journal or manuscript or *écriture* begin on the cover of the book with the words *Alibi: A Novel.* Since "alibi" means "elsewhere," its range of significations include "absence, non-existence, non-attendance, absenteeism" (*Roget's Thesaurus* 59). Like Dorf (not only) himself, the writing both is, and is not, where/what it is supposed to be. As Dorfendorf (I? he?) writes: "Birthday today. Meaning, five days ago. I cross out *I am* and write *He is* . . . He . . . I. . . . What does it matter? I am, he is, at last, this morning, trying to catch up" (51).

In the following passage, Karen reflects on the status of the I/he figure of Dorfendorf. Given the relation between alibi and absence, they are especially telling lines. "'We all live by our alibis, don't we Dorf?' But she didn't wait for an answer, 'We were somewhere else when it happened. Or should have been. Or shouldn't have been'" (125). Her words suggest that we all live by our absences from ourselves, that we might just, as Lacan has said, think where we are not. "What else is there but the dream" Dorf asks (35). The connections between "alibi" and "absence" suggest a relation between narrator and text. For "it" to happen in a text, we (as narrators) have to be somewhere else than where it is happening. To write is to have an alibi for the events of the text. We cannot both live the scene and have it in writing: "We cannot have what we want, and we hurt" (55).

But an alibi may also be a plea, made by a suspect, that when an alleged act took place s/he was elsewhere. The narrator (Dorfendorf? Kroetsch?) of (the) *Alibi* is always pleading that when the act of writing took place he (I?) too was absent. "He," the novel argues, had an alibi. Identity is posited as an alibi for being lost. Even sexual identity is an absence. The name of the "Dwarf" figure "Manny," is a feminization of the word "man." And his position in the grammar of the narrative is a dislocating one: "imagine my surprise, even my horror, when the woman or girl turned around and proved to be, not only a male, but a dwarf as well" (111). Dorf says that Manny "looked, for all the world in spite of his being male, like a miniature of Karen Strike" (113). "Dwarf," who resembles "Dorf" in name, makes us consider the question (for it certainly is one) of the sexual identity of the Dwarf, Dorf, and Julie in the following passage:

> It was the marvellous possibilities of our little triangle that gave me no rest from desire. I felt not the slightest touch of jealousy. Indeed, by pretending just slightly that Manny was Karen, with his head of perfect blond hair, I was able to add a further dimension to our already outrageous joy. I truly felt no jealousy. I was able to write in my journal exactly on each day those two blind words: he . . . I. And what did it matter, the slightest difference? We were together and as one. We were two as one and three as one and each of us, one as three, isosceles in our splendor. (130)

Just as *Alibi* is an alibi for a narrative, so, too, is sexual identity an alibi.

Dorf makes a point of telling us that days pass before he transcribes events into text and a further passage of time occurs before the journal/text becomes novel/text. There is no immediate writing:

> I began to imagine entries in my journal. . . . I'm going to keep a journal, I'm going to love two women, I'm going to tell the truth. Life is unendurable. The trouble is, I enjoy it. Yesterday made sense, I can see that now, but today doesn't. Maybe that is what journals are about. (39)

This self-consciousness is what always goes on in a D(w)orfed text: "I must let this entry stand as I originally wrote it . . . I have emended and summarized elsewhere only to establish a narrative account whose clarity matches my insight" (100). But, as Karen recognizes, Dorf's insight does not precede the text. "He " is created out of its writing: "You invent yourself, each time you sit down to make an entry, and I feel envy, watching you" (61).

In contrast, Karen Strike seeks to tell the truth and so does not *tell* anything. Karen Strike ("almost frightening, that word, Strike . . . STRIKE. I print it in capitals") has "a killer instinct of her own" (51). She wants to make the perfect documentary by "making notes on the goddamned world" (16). She wants to make *the* world. "She" is not happy with the excerpts. While Dorf suggests she should "Fake the real," her "Randy" cameraman says "The real would suffice" (51). Like documentary film-making, the search for the source of health and of healing is "a kind of absence, a reduction to nothing" (52). *The* spa is not there.

For Dorf, finding the perfect spa, healing the wound, would be impossible and undesirable (it would literally put an end to desire). Such a finding, such a final collection, would put an end to signification:

> "People never tell," I said, "that's the way it is. They can't."
> "They should," Karen said.
> "They should, they should," I answered. (27)

Although he resolves again and again to tell the truth, Dorf realizes that "the" truth would have to be a lie: "I had to make up part of the story. After my resolve that I would, finally, on my birthday, begin to tell the whole truth, nothing but. Because at forty-six you aren't really forty-six; you're into your forty-seventh year. The number, that too, isn't and is a lie." "Tell me some more," says Karen (25), and we with her.

One of the most telling passages in the text is the opening one, which makes a kind of uncanny sense only after an initial reading of *Alibi*: "Most men, I suppose, are secretly pleased to learn their wives have taken lovers; I am now able to confess I was" (7). These words invoke the contradictory and destabilized "I" that we find later figured as William William Dorfendorf, the figure of agent and subject. If "I" am now able to confess "I" was, I am absent from my former self, and I can act and speak now based on my readings of the past self. I have an alibi for not being who "I" say "I" am.

Certainties about self, text, event, truth, are all undermined in Kroetsch's *Alibi*. If there are events in this anti-narrative they are textual events, scenes of writing and rewriting. By multiplying and problematizing the identity of the narrator and positing many levels of narrative as scenes of writing, the text subverts an explanation of its construction; the text is about the processes of construction of self and text. Descriptions become de/scriptions—un/writings or unravellings. *Alibi* self-reflexively informs the reader of its deconstructive potential and offers within itself a narratology that plays with the most seductive elements of deconstructive theory. But *Alibi* also deconstructs the assumptions of the practitioner of narratology—one who assumes the coherence of the writing/reading self, of the written/already-read text. *Alibi* is useful for feminism because, like Kroetsch's most recent poetry, it offers a dislocating and (in all senses of the word) disarming theory of subjectivity.

CHAPTER EIGHT

On Sending Yourself: Kroetsch and the New Autobiography

> June 4.
>
> No mail at all from you. None. I talk to myself. I begin to suspect I am writing these letters to myself, writing myself the poem of you.
>
> —Kroetsch, "Letters to Salonika," *Advice to My Friends*

> 25/3/85
>
> This is a poem I didn't write. And not because I wasn't writing. And not because it isn't a poem. I'm beside myself.
>
> —Kroetsch, *Excerpts from the Real World*

> I didn't mean to change. But he did.
>
> —Kroetsch, "After Paradise," *Completed Field Notes*

As I argued in Chapter Three, Kroetsch's continuing poem *Field Notes* is a glossary of fragments. In its appropriation of the discourse of archaeology, it challenges notions of linear order, coherence, chronology, finality. Robert Lecker speaks of *Field Notes* as a "collective poem in process—a site continually being unearthed" (*Robert Kroetsch* 125). The most recent supplements to the continuing poem—*Advice to My Friends* (1985), *Excerpts from the Real World* (1986), and "After Paradise" (1987), now collected with the earlier long poems in the outrageously entitled *Completed Field Notes* (1989)—offer further unearthings of the site, particularly the autobiographical site upon which they, uneasily, locate themselves.

In her reading of the notion of "self" in *Field Notes*, Shirley Neuman argues persuasively that the relation of autobiography to Kroetsch's texts is always a difficult one. Citing remarks Kroetsch made on autobiography in 1981, Neuman's 1983 essay follows the "movement from what Kroetsch calls the '*language* problem' of writing autobiography, through the definition of autobiography as freeing us from Self, to the gloss on that statement: 'Saying "I" is a wonderful release from I'" ("Allow Self, Portraying Self" 107). In a footnote to her 1984 essay, "Figuring the Reader," Neuman conjectures that "[w]hat began as multiplication of the self in personae and roles of the 'I' has become increasingly straightforward in recent poems like 'The Frankfurt *Hauptbahnhof*' where the 'I' of the poem shares the undisguised anecdotes and experiences of its author" (194).

Kroetsch's recent texts continue to interrogate notions of "I," experience, and anecdote—the *autos*, *bios*, and *graphia* of classical autobiography. But asked in a recent interview with Kristjana Gunnars if "writing your poem with your life" meant writing "pure autobiography," Kroetsch replied "I have grave doubts about the whole possibility of autobiography. We're too busy lying to ever be autobiographical, I think. You write the poem with your life by not creating a safe boundary between poety and life" (67). While many theories of autobiography assume there is always a safe boundary between poetry and life, for Kroetsch, "[i]t would be nice if there sometimes were a clear boundary, but in fact the two keep spilling back and forth; exchanging" (Gunnars 67).

Sidonie Smith's recent study of women's autobiography locates three sets of assumptions upon which the writing and reading of autobiography have been based: one assumes autobiography is a subcategory of biography, that "truthfulness" in autobiography is "a matter of biographical facticity" (4); another agonizes over the questions inherent in self-representation: "autobiography is understood to be a process through which the autobiographer struggles to shape an 'identity' out of amorphous subjectivity" (5); a third attends to the function of reading in the creation of autobiography. Janet Varner Gunn argues that moments of reading "produce" the autobiographical text in a number of ways. The autobiographer reads his or her life, and the reader of the autobiographical text, in an encounter with the text, rereads his or her life by association (8).

Compelling as our desire to represent ourselves remains, much contemporary thought participates in an equally compelling desire to eradicate the notion of self. Film theory has drawn our attention to the problematical assumptions underlying approaches to autobiography which conjoin the roles of author, narrator, and protagonist "with the same individual occupying a position both in the context, the associated 'scene of writing,' and within the text itself" (Bruss 300). Elizabeth Bruss notes simply that there is "no real cinematic equivalent for autobiography": "The unity of subjectivity and subject matter—the implied identity of author, narrator, and protagonist on which classical autobiography depends—seems to be shattered by film" (297). The "self" produced in film is dispersed across a range of positions, including those of the person appearing on the screen, visible and recorded, and the person filming the person on the screen, invisible, behind the camera's eye, and unrecorded (Bruss 297). Like many contemporary theorists of autobiography, including Michael Sprinker, Jacques Derrida, and Gregory Ulmer, Bruss assumes that "autobiography as we know it is at an end" and turns her attention to "autobiography as we do not know it" (Olney 22).

In a provocative essay entitled "The Post-Age," Ulmer describes Derrida's unknown version of autobiography in *The Post Card* as a "new autobiography" which "has little to do with confession or expression" (46). In Derrida's words, when I write (autobiography), "I address myself to you, somewhat as if I were sending myself, never certain of seeing it come back, that which is destined for me" (*The Post Card* 45). Kroetsch's most recent supplements to the continuing poem offer other examples of autobiography as we do not know it, autobiography that has little to do with expression or confession.

Kroetsch's recent "autobiographical" texts both elide what Neuman speaks of as "the traditional distinction between the author (writer) and narrator (aspect of the written) in favor of writing" ("Figuring the Reader" 194) and figure a multiple subjectivity inhabiting the most seemingly "personal" of written forms: the journal, post card, love letter, note. Because these forms of writing assume a "marginal status in the discourse of knowledge" and an "undecidability" because of their "informality" and "autobiographical component" ("The Post-Age" 41), they may be considered as letters, in Ulmer's sense. The letter's strategy, says Ulmer, is "disguised self-address." Like Derrida, who "writes the post cards to himself (the code is between me and myself) by means of 'apostrophe'" (Ulmer 42), Kroetsch suspects he is "writing these letters" to himself

("Letters to Salonika" 53). Kroetsch "sends himself" in writing only to "receive himself" as another: "we are not where we were" ("Spending the Morning on the Beach" (33). The "self" represented in the most recent long poems exists only in and as displacement: "What was it I said I said? I said to Laura" ("Delphi: Commentary," *Advice to My Friends* 104).

"The Frankfurt *Hauptbahnhof*" is an especially powerful articulation of the writing of autobiography as a dislocating experience of the self "facing" a difference within—"I tried to reconstruct the occasion of my meeting with my double":

> 10 . . .
> The voice of that man who directed me onto the right train, the train that would take me to Koblenz, where I would then transfer onto another train and proceed to Trier, to give a talk on Canadian writing (and I gave the talk), had been exactly my own.
> 11
> like, I
> mean
> (*Advice to My Friends* 126-27)

For Kroetsch, "I" cannot be myself because "I" am constituted "like" a poem, "and cannot hear except by indirection. We can only guess the poem by encountering (by being surprised by) its double" (*Advice to My Friends* 125).

Many other poems in both *Advice* and *Excerpts* offer the poem as (always already) fictional post card, love letter, journal entry. But consider first an even later poem, "Spending the Morning on the Beach," in which the speaker self-consciously considers

> The poem as quotation . . .
> The poem as evasion.
> The poem as resignation.
> The poem as a net
> that drowns fish.
> The poem as a postcard
> sent directly to the sun.
> The poem as POET TREE.
> (40)

The post card poem as a place to "*hang* a self" (a "poet tree") offers a theory of autobiography which undermines traditional "confidence in the referentiality of language and a corollary confidence in the authenticity of the self" (Sidonie Smith 5). The new autobiography is, as Kroetsch's poems indicate, simultaneously self-affirming *and* self-effacing, in the most literal sense. As Paul Smith argues, "the 'me' can be written only as if it were somewhere else" (108). Written with/in the conventions of the "letter," these poems exploit what is always the precondition of writing autobiography—the absence of sender and receiver: "the text takes on a life of its own, and the self that was not really in existence in the beginning is in the end merely a matter of text and has nothing whatever to do with an authorizing author" (Olney 22).

Consider "Letters to Salonika," written by the poet at home to the absent beloved: "Sometimes I think this going away of yours has hurt me beyond all repair. I am not myself and cannot ever be again. I am my own emptiness, trying to fill my emptiness with words" (*Advice* 46). Or "Postcards From China," written by the poet away from home and sent back to his (he hopes) reading daughters. Or the ten parts of the prose poem *Excerpts from the Real World* made up of dated fragments, some of them written, Kroetsch says, "before the date got there because I couldn't wait" (Gunnars 57). These are all poem as "contrived diary" (Gunnars 57), cryptic post card message, unposted letter, lost telegram, incomplete note.

Advice to My Friends and *Excerpts from the Real World* are letters, excerpts from the "real world" which, with recognizable names—Eli Mandel, Fred Wah, Smaro (Kamboureli), Michael Ondaatje—dates—March 1982, the spring of '76, December 6, 1983—and places—Slocan Valley, Kootenay River, China—locate us in a real world only to dislocate us from the possibility of the real:

> if we could just get a hold of it,
> catch aholt, some kind of a line,
> if the sun was a tennis ball or something
> but it ain't, the impossible thing is the sun.
> ("Advice to My Friends,"
> *Advice to My Friends* 9)

If only, as an excerpt from *Excerpts* says, we could go "to a place where things are only what they are. Or, with the barest exception, something else, but only just something else, hardly"; a place where "words are not allowed at all" (63). To paraphrase a piece of advice in *Advice*, to desire an end to desiring language is to desire language (65).

Kroetsch's new autobiography makes fictions of autobiography and autobiography of fiction. In contrast to the usual autobiographical situation in which, as Ulmer says, "the author unwittingly reveals himself while attending to the presentation of information" (46), the selves that are revealed in the "new autobiography" contradict one another and tell on each other:

> But I could see he had forgotten the year of his birth. He's showing his age. And then he added, suddenly, powerfully, "I've never been here myself." And the voice, Laura; you should have heard him. But I was puzzled by his statement. "I've never been here myself." And there he was, right beside me. ("Postcards from China," *Advice to My Friends* 82)

Even the Elias Canetti epigraph to *Advice to My Friends* locates the "I" in the third person: "I hesitated until he vanished from sight, then I started off, taking the same road as he." As Barthes directs us in *Roland Barthes by Roland Barthes*, "all this must be considered as if spoken by a character in a novel—or rather by several characters" (119). The singular "I" becomes literally unspeakable.

Consider the following transcription of the dialogue between Kroetsch and Gunnars I referred to earlier:

> KG: Are you then writing this poem with your life?
> RK: That's right. I think life itself is circumlocution.
> KG: Around what?
> RK: It's the unspeakable. If we're talking around anything, I don't like to name it, and I suppose it's the unnameable or the unspeakable. The only reason we like poetry is because it does attempt to deal with the unknowable. (56)

Kroetsch's words are not unlike those of Beckett's "character" in *The Unnameable* who says, "I like to think I occupy the centre, but nothing is less certain. In a sense I would be better off at the circumference. . . . From centre to circumference in any case it is a far cry and I may well be situated somewhere between the two":

> This voice that speaks, knowing that it lies, indifferent to what it says . . . not listening to itself but to the silence that it breaks . . . is it one? . . . It issues from me, it fills me, it clamours against my

> wall, it is not mine, I can't stop it, I can't prevent it, from tearing me, rocking me, assailing me. It is not mine. (51)

As for Beckett, so too for Kroetsch: "I am in words, made of words, other's words" (*The Unnameable* 386); "I am my own emptiness trying to fill my emptiness with words" (*Advice to My Friends* 46). But Kroetsch's work stresses the play, not the anguish: "SELF-PORTRAIT OF POET or THROWING IN THE TOWEL, EH?" ("Spending the Morning on the Beach" 39).

Many of the poems in *Advice to My Friends* confront the ways we "are" in others' words by exposing the different "language codes" ("Mile Zero," *Advice* 34) within which our sense of "self" is articulated, the multiple fictions that make us real: "I find myself reading the old guys now" (*Advice to My Friends* 22). The "piecemeal sonnet[s]" (*Advice* 9) in the long poem "Advice to My Friends" locate themselves "piecemeal" within the colloquial discourse of the Western prairie farmer: "if we could just get a hold of it, / catch aholt, some kind of a line" (9); the sports commentator: "Morenz makes a breakaway down the ice. / He fakes to the left; he draws out the goalie" (13); the journalist: "In a delightful ceremony at the bride's / boarding house in Victoria, the nuptial / event is consummated. The family / of Mr. Morenz is not in attendance" (14). But the certainty of each mode of speaking is called into question by its interaction with the others. The lexicon of the hockey game, for instance—"player," "lines," "masks"—intersects with the lexicon of the poet: "The hockey player, the artist: they both have // strong wrists" (*Advice* 15). Each way of talking in and about the world rewrites the others.

Excerpts from the Real World is a particularly self-conscious meditation on the place of the subject of autobiography in what Derrida would call a post-postal era: the "I" is "an echo without prior sound until you, silently, wrote 'I am counting on my fingers to remember you.' If only you had got my name right" (69). The "I" is dislocated both by linguistic play—"Praxis makes perfect, you tell me. But I'm Dedalus on my feet" (45); "Two loves halve I, you wrote on your last postcard" (43)—and by the contradictory language codes within which s/he speaks:

> "But most of all I luv you cuz yr you." If you see what I mean. (29)

> But most of all I love you. The rabbits have no shadows of their own. The mirror falls into its own error. (31)

Excerpts repeatedly gestures toward the lack of presence of the speaking self: "Even as I lay down, I heard myself walking away" (31); "This is a poem I didn't write. And not because I wasn't writing" (24); "I did not intend to enter the story" (19). And perhaps most memorably, given the implied link between writing and subjectivity in the following metaphors: "I am a stranger's hand" (23).

The last poem in *Advice to My Friends*—"envoi (to begin with)"—offers a telling commentary on both *Excerpts from the Real World* and *Advice to My Friends*:

> There is no real
> world, my friends.
> Why not, then,
> let the stars
> shine in our bones?
> (143)

If this poem offers a "final" bit of "advice," what is it? How can we let the stars shine in our bones? One of the "Letters to Salonika" tells us that a letter is sometimes "a star that fell. Sometimes it is a rock, a stone" (59). Already the "envoi" sends us off to other letters. As envoi to *Advice to My Friends*, the poem literally prefaces ["(to begin with)"] *Excerpts from the Real World* in the *Completed Field Notes* edition of the long poems.

"Envoi (to begin with)" sends us off to many other letters, including Derrida's *La carte postale*, the lengthy first part of which (nearly half of the book) is called "Envois." Alan Bass's translation includes a useful gloss on the word "envoi." I cite particularly relevant sections of it here:

> *Envoi, envoyer: envoyer*, to send, is derived from the Latin *inviare*, to send on the way. . . . The noun *envoi* can mean the action of sending (*envoi de lettres*: the sending of letters) . . . something that is sent (especially in the senses of message, missive, or dispatch), the concluding stanza of a ballad that typically serves as a dedication, the lines handwritten by the author of a book as part of a dedication. . . . Both "invoice" and *envoi* are homonyms of "in voice" and *en voix*: the "Envois" are written in many voices. . . . The reflexive verb *s'envoyer* is particularly

> important. It can mean to send oneself, transitively or intransitively. In the latter sense, one might say that if one sends oneself, then one's en-voy (also *en-voi*) or representative has to be one's double or ghost. (xx-xxi)

Recall that the advice given in "The Frankfurt *Hauptbahnhof*" concerns the possibility of "sending oneself," of being sent by a double, of writing autobiography:

> And when the man
> came up beside me,
> when he spoke
> over my left shoulder,
> telling me I was (I was
> surprised) getting
> onto the wrong train,
> pointing me right, I
> hardly noticed; I had
> no time, even, to say
> thank you   (Like the guy said.)
> (118)

To write this form of autobiography is to meet with the double which confirms, not identity, but difference within: "Like me, he was pushing a cart with his luggage on it. he was wearing a green corduroy jacket, like mine. he was slightly younger than I, but only slightly, a matter of a year or two" (121). But the doppelganger, the "gone stranger" (121) is not me: "I never/ wear a hat" (127).

The "new autobiography" interrogates the place of the subject of/in knowledge and considers subjectivity a textual site of contradiction. The usual situation of autobiography is re-versed and becomes what Manina Jones, borrowing from a quoted phrase in *Excerpts*, calls a "chaotic, strung-along multi-verse" (123). "The author" becomes *L'autre* ("I'm not myself today" [*Excerpts* 15]). Information is not "pre-sent": "Everything recurs (more or less). Consider, for instance, spring. Or transmission problems" (*Excerpts* 35). But the problems in "transmission," the disjunctions between signifier and signified that keep us from telling, make it possible always to tell otherwise: "It's a kind of circular tension, where you're making an utterance that then turns around and utters against itself, makes fun of itself and it comes back full circle. Circular, as in circum-locution, and the silent poet somewhere in the middle, and you keep looking for him. . . . The guy who goes out at night and digs holes—makes gaps" (Gunnars 57).

In an interview with Shirley Neuman, Kroetsch articulates the theory of this "new autobiography," the theory behind his practice of writing/letters:

> against the idea of truth, I would posit the idea of play or game. Once you're into play or game you're so self-conscious of the artificiality of it. The more I write the more I do feel the business of being taken over at some point by language, or the form, the genre. ("Unearthing Language" 238)

In speaking, we are always already "into play or game." We construct ourselves and, in rereading those constructions, tell ourselves who we are differently: "Last night, late, the trees outside my window were holding hands. I miss you, apparently" (*Excerpts from the Real World* 30). The self is a "self-portrait," a "found object, signed by yours truly, as we all know . . . given a name by another, appropriated" ("Spending the Morning on the Beach" 36).

Both *Advice to My Friends* and *Excerpts from the Real World* are extended meditations on an unwittingly accurate observation Robert Brunne made in 1330: "bot as I herd telle I say myn auys" (*The Story of England*). The "advice" that I say is my own is always what I "herd telle": "(Like the guy said)" (118), "(and so the story goes)" (119), "[what happens / in the margin / is what happens]" (119). Like notation, giving advice is "prediction, / a saying (assaying) of / what will be said":

> (or so
> (the
> (story
> (goes
> (*Advice* 117)

The way the story goes is the way "we" go. But we are not completely "written" by the stories that tell us. As Richard Poirier asks in "Writing Off the Self,"

> If it is agreed that human beings are a consequence of "the arrangements of knowledge," and not the other way around, what then is to be said of the evidence that human beings have the

> capacity to wish themselves radically other than what they are? (120)

The new autobiography affirms the self in its desire to speak otherwise because it foregrounds the act of saying as always already a trying to say (assaying) that permits the possibility of change.

I cite the second half of Kroetsch's comments on autobiography, the first half of which Neuman analyzed at length, because they can suggest the theory of autobiography I find at work (play) in Kroetsch's recent texts. He says,

> Autobiography, as I conceive it, is paradoxical: it frees us from self. Saying *I* is a wonderful release from *I*, isn't it? Language, then, as signifier, frees me into a new relationship with signified. Autobiography conceived this way can free us from solipsism, can free us from the humanistic temptation to coerce the world. (*Labyrinths of the Voice* 209)

Frank Lentricchia conceives of autobiography in this way in a recent article. By constructing a similar reading of the writing of "I" as an entering into the play of the signifier, he considers autobiography, indeed any writing, "not as a space for the preservation of identity and the assertion of voice, but as a labyrinth" into which "I" can "escape," "lose myself," or "write yourself off, as it were" ("Anatomy of a Jar" 400).

Both "Letters to Salonika" and "Postcards from China" are, for example, attempts to write the self off. But they do not produce the kind of voice, which Poirier locates in Foucault and Nietzsche, which "seems to assume that we who listen, like those who speak, are somehow *more* than human" (115). If, as Neuman suggests, in recent poems "the 'I' of the poem shares the undisguised anecdotes and experiences of its author" ("Figuring the Reader" 194), in writing the poems, the reader, like the subject in the poems, consistently encounters the double that, in the "real" world, is elided. Consider, for example, the "despair of the poet on meeting / reality" (63) in the following passage from "Letters to Salonika":

> Lying on your side of the bed this morning I looked at the frame of the mirror on your dresser. Making strange. The shaved wood. Needing oil now. The curved lines, in the wood around the glass. The mirror holding in its stare the room. Yesterday, phoning you,

> expecting you to be in Salonika, back from Athens. You on your quest, me here at home. (*Advice to My Friends* 63)

But we become "familiar" to ourselves only by "making strange." If the poet can write "Wednesday, I'm up at 4:00 am. I was up at 4:00, it's 5:00 now" ("Letters to Salonika" 45), the linguistic construction of the sentence itself points out the ways that "I" "am" by *not* being myself.

In writing letters, in appropriating selves, we never are the selves we write we are: "I receive a letter from you and it's so old that you are already someone else, the letter is out of joint with the reality that I imagine. A problem in form, a dislocation that is real" (*Advice to My Friends* 61). In "Letters to Salonika" the poet gestures toward what will be the subject of "Postcards from China" and says, "I do not have enough stories of China to be able to imagine the China that I should be imagining" (*Advice to My Friends* 58). Our experience is possible on the basis of the stories we know. What the poet imagines are roads in China turn out not to be roads. He has no language for his experience and so does not have the experience: "I am in China without a language. What I saw from the sky was roads that weren't roads; I saw the irrigation system for watering the land and from up in the sky I thought I saw roads . . . and so in a sense they were roads" (*Advice to My Friends* 76).

China becomes a metaphor for the "experience" of the subject in language: "China is a garden and a maze" (*Advice to My Friends* 81). It is a place of dislocation, of vacillation, of Derridean *différance*. The "translator," Mr. Wong, exemplifies what can only be described as the ex/position of the subject, "in love with words and the way they try to buck him off" (78). The maze, the garden, the labyrinth, the place of self and other, man and woman, is the place within which we are all caught and yet the maze can potentially "tease us out of our habitual ways" (88). Even as the poet attempts to maintain identity, he finds "I was lost and I was trying to find a post office. I wanted to mail you a card I had written" (88).

If Kroetsch's poems are letters from the poet to himself, they are self-conscious struggles with the autobiographical "I," not as a present self, but as an always already "sent" or even "re-sent" (recent) self. The "I" of the poet is, as "he"/the father is at the end of "Delphi: Commentary," a story his "daughters" can *tell* their friends

(*Advice to My Friends* 112). Created in the reception of letters, the "I" is both spoken by and speaks the writer as reader as writer. All we *can* give our friends is advice; we are stories; we tell (on) each other. As examples of the new autobiography, the most recent supplements to Kroetsch's continuing poem are, to borrow a linguistic innovation from Teresa de Lauretis, a(-)sendings which, by exposing the conventions of autobiography, challenge the possibility of sending a(-)self without sending another. They seek "to establish practices in which 'I' may no longer exist in the same way but nonetheless cannot escape my own participation" (Bruss 320). As Kroetsch acknowledged recently, "I like symbolic significance, but I also like the sense that we eat real carrots and we eat real potatoes, and one of the pleasures in life is fiddling around in the kitchen slicing onions" (Gunnars 61). In these poems, Kroetsch figures the contrary subject, "a subject, therefore, not unified but rather multiple, and not so much divided as contradicted" (de Lauretis, *Technologies of Gender* 2):

> RK: What's knowable is already boring in a certain way. We want to go to that edge, where something is still unknown. And we're still full of surprises, discoveries, impossibilities, and contradictions. (Gunnars 56)

As for de Lauretis, so too for Kroetsch; not only the fictions, but also the contradictions, make us real.

In /Conclusion . . .

In/Conclusion . . .

> Fluid and in motion, feminism is an assertion of values that, like Gallop's concept of identity, "must be continually assumed and immediately called into question" [*The Daughter's Seduction* xii]. From this perspective, there will never be *a theory* of feminist criticism; rather, feminist criticism will be a theorizing process, guided perhaps by an ethical dream of relationships between others. As one who dreams of what is not now, though fervently sought, I must refuse to close this question, preferring instead to write in/conclusion.
>
> —Elizabeth Meese

Elizabeth Meese draws a useful parallel between Gallop's concept of identity—what I have been speaking of as feminism's doubled notion of subjectivity—and feminism generally. Because reading, too, is a "theorizing process," I am tempted to write under Meese's sign of "in/conclusion." In doing so, I reverse the question of this book, how does Kroetsch's work offer a feminist theory of subjectivity, and ask, how does an awareness of this theory of subjectivity—of differences within—translate into feminist literary-critical practice? In asking the question, I shall consider an article by Alice Jardine which, in its discussion of the neologism "gynesis," gestures towards such feminist practice.

In her preface to *The Future of Difference*, a 1980 anthology of feminist literary theory and criticism, Jardine raises the question, "what is the process, product and function" of feminist scholarship? What can feminism—especially the feminisms struggling with questions raised by French theory—*do*? "Gynesis," a 1982 article in *Diacritics*, gestures toward a feminist practice informed by contemporary French theory. It attempts to bring together the questions raised by postmodernism with feminism. In an often anguished, always self-conscious, reading of both Anglo-American feminism and French feminist theory, Jardine speaks of a series of phases within feminist thinking which takes into account the work of both groups. These stages are not unlike the feminist "generations" Kristeva speaks of in "Women's Time."

For Jardine, the "fundamental feminist gesture" is "an analysis (and critique) of fictional representations of women (characters) in men's and women's writing" ("Gynesis" 56). Within this feminist impulse she identifies two stages which are very like Showalter's distinction between feminist critique and gynocriticism, between: (1) women who write books about men's books; and (2) women who write books about women's books. Both of these feminist practices, she says, rest on assumptions about identity, authority, and authorship, and are called into question by the contemporary French inquiry into the implications of postmodernism.

Feminism, as Jardine notes, is inherited from "the humanist and rationalist eighteenth century" and is "traditionally about a group of human beings in history whose identity is defined by that history's representation of sexual decidability" (58). In a consideration of the meanings generated by the phrase "Men in Feminism," Jardine discovers that in the French *Littré* (1892) the word "feminism" "was sometimes used to refer to a *man* exhibiting feminine characteristics":

> More precisely, it states: "feminism: a break in the development of a man around adolescence which gives him certain feminine attributes." And, unbelievably, one also finds: "Feminist: a man who is attracted to women"! (*Men in Feminism* 54)

In English, there is no mention of men. "Simply," she writes, "(1846) 'Femininism [*sic*]: the state of being feminine' or 'a feminine or woman's word or expression' or (1851) 'Feminism: The qualities of females'" (55).

Notably, in both the French and English traditions, "feminism" is a word which, whether permitting "men" or not, assumes that there are stable differences between men and women and sees human beings as fully unified gendered subjects. If, in nineteenth-century France, a man could be a "feminist" because he had "certain feminine attributes," there was still no question that "he" was "a man." Similarly, although the meanings of "feminine" and "woman" were elided in the English definition—feminism was defined as "a feminine or woman's word or expression"—"woman" was, nonetheless, a stable, unquestionable position from which to speak.

Postmodernism—in Canada, writing like Kroetsch's—in its challenges to identity, representation, truth, has called entirely into question the assumptions upon which such a notion of "feminism" is based. Jardine suggests that *gynesis* is a product of an intersection between postmodernism and feminism. I would locate gynesis within a signifying space that involves, among other things, "a total reconceptualization of difference (beyond contradiction), self-consciously throwing both sexes into a metonymic confusion of gender" ("Gynesis" 60). Yet "Gynesis" offers an alternative, specifically feminist, practice which arises out of contemporary French theories of language and subjectivity.

Elaine Marks tells the difference between Anglo-American and French "feminisms" by arguing that "American feminists emphasize the oppression of woman as sexual identity while the French feminists emphasize the repression of difference and alterity in the signifying practices of the West" (qtd. in *The Future of Difference* xxvi). Jardine hopes to find the sensitive point of contact between "American feminist thought—a primarily ethical discourse as prescription for action—and a certain French emphasis on the human subject's inscription in culture through language" (*The Future of Difference* xxxvi).

I locate Jardine's practice within a feminist signifying space because, while it moves away from the first stage feminist question—Who am I?—which implies a false singularity and unity of the speaking subject, it asks new feminist questions: Who is speaking? What is the effect of appropriating a range of subject positions? What are the implications of the contemporary theoretical assertion that the "I" speaks only as a difference within itself, as both self and other, the same and different, as a site of contradictions? For this signifying space Jardine suggests "a new name," "a believable neologism: *gynesis*":

> the putting into discourse of "woman" as that process beyond the Cartesian subject, the Dialectics of Representation, or Man's truth. The object produced by this process is neither a person nor a thing but a horizon, that towards which the process is tending: a *gynema*. This *gynema* is a reading effect, a woman-in-effect, never stable, without identity. ("Gynesis" 58)

To consider the methodological implications of this theory of gynesis—a theory which can open up a space for another feminism—I will reread the Jardine text of "Gynesis"—a text that enacts the process which the theory of gynesis argues for.

"Gynesis" begins with a radical questioning of the speaker's subject position and a recognition that the "I" is indeed several. "She" begins by deferring "her own" words to those of Paul de Man, who writes that "when addressing two cultures the distressing question as to who should be exploiting whom is bound to arise":

> In Paris, after almost three years of working closely with feminists and others, I am no longer sure either whom I am "observing" or who my "others" are. Given that inbetween [*sic*] state, I would like to begin with the title of the MLA Special Session for which this paper was originally written: "New Directions in Feminist Critical Theories in France and the Francophone World." ("Gynesis" 55)

"Jardine" refers to her "own" experience only to indicate how much "identity" is subject to shift. Moving from this "inbetween state" into the argument, "she" again defers her authority to speak by calling into question the received language—the title of the MLA session in which she originally spoke.

Notably, she takes as her second point of departure a *textual* point—the *title* of the MLA Special Session for which the paper was written—and proceeds to question each of the terms in the title: "new directions," "feminist," "critical." It is "unclear," she argues, whether there are any "new directions" in French "feminist" thought right now. In fact, the French MLF (Mouvement de Libération des Femmes) *is* the "psychoanalysis and politics" group which is deliberately anti-feminist. The term French feminism is thus a highly suspect one. If it is not the practising, studying, "invisible feminists" hard at work behind the scenes in France, and if it is not the visible theorists, Cixous, Kristeva, Lemoin-Luccioni, who see themselves as "beyond" feminism, what is feminism in France? Where is it going?

I have not yet remarked on the other column of text in the Jardine article, a column which includes a sketched figure of a woman, "chipper"—dressed, significantly, as a "referee." The other column of text includes words like "ineligible receiver," "illegal pass," "touchdown," written below "her" and the gestures "she" makes. The second column interacts tellingly with the written text. It is another gesture which undermines the authority of the speaker. This cartooned "chipper" is, according to the written part of that text, and quite paradoxically, given the fact that she is dressed as a referee, "officially speaking." She takes the discourse of a man's game and tells the difference: she signifies more than words can say. The text of the article we call "Gynesis" by Alice Jardine is, similarly, a gesture toward a new methodology for rereading the men's language, our father's words, "his" field notes.

Jardine's paper dances around the question of truth. She sees the new directions in contemporary French thought as attempts to come to terms with postmodernism as a philosophical and aesthetic movement which dislodges the position and intentionality of the author, disrupts linear narrative, and dismantles sexual identity. Each of these challenges is, she sees, a challenge to feminism. These tendencies in the postmodern text and in poststructuralist theory have important implications for Anglo-American feminism because, as Jardine writes, "an analysis (and critique) of fictional representations of women (characters) in men's and women's writing" (56) takes for granted the possibility of representation, character, sexual identity.

The disappearance of the author, the move away from mimesis, and the dissolving of sexual identity are closely linked to the process of reconceptualizing the subject, the dialectics of representation, and man's truth, which is gynesis. If, as theorists of psychoanalysis and deconstruction have argued, it is not "I" but language which speaks, and both the concept of the author and the Cartesian subject are disturbed, the "appearance of the gynema in a written text" is "noticed only by the woman (feminist) reader" (58): "If an autonomous 'I' or 'he' can no longer exist then only an anonymous 'she' will be seen to—as Heidegger might say—ex-sist" (60). Or, as Jardine notes elsewhere, " 'woman' may become intrinsic to an entire conceptual system, without being 'about' women—much less 'about' feminism" (58).

The "subject" in the kind of critical practice Jardine seeks is "woman" in this sense. S/he is a self which is always already an/other. Like the speaking subject, "she" is partial, anti-universalizing, multiply divided within. As "woman," the plurality of the "I" *is* its specificity. The position of woman is the position of lack which offers the possibility of subjectivity: "a man becomes a woman when he writes or, if not, he does not 'write' (in the radical sense of *écriture*) what he writes" (57).

Jardine's notion of gynesis reacts against a whole set of phallogocentric assumptions about the possibility of wholeness, unity, and integrity. It is beyond the "dialectics of representation." "Woman's" position is the ex/position of the subject. It is the place that is out of place from which we all speak when we speak. "Woman" speaks in ecstatic documents, to borrow a phrase from Kroetsch. To recognize the tentativeness of our positions as always already ex/positions is to see that the "tears in the fabric of men's truth" offer us a glimpse of that impossible and yet necessary notion of a feminism beyond feminism.

I began this digression toward Jardine by asking, how do we move from this doubled theory of subjectivity to a feminist critical practice? I reread my own question by noting the significations of the words "from" and "to," both of which are metaphors of address, destination, communication. These are metaphors that Kroetsch's work calls into question. *Excerpts from the Real World*, "Postcards from China," and *Advice to My Friends*, for example, use these words and place them under erasure. In a Kroetsch text, both sender and receiver are postulated, but not present. "The circulation of letters by mail" in Kroetsch's texts as in Derrida's, is a metaphor "as acute and serviceable to deconstruction as speaking was to philosophy of consciousness" (Smith and Kerrigan x). We cannot move simply or easily from one position to another. Like our origins, our destinations are always other than we expect; there is no express(ive) route.

The project of this book has been to locate, in Kroetsch's work, textual moments at which the possibility of "sending oneself," of speaking as a unified, gendered, male or female subject is dissolved, or at least deferred. To discover the contradictions within logocentric philosophy and the assumptions of speech—presence, meaning, intention—is to locate a post-logocentric philosophy of letter-writing. The theory of subjectivity feminist readers find in Kroetsch's work is inscribed within a letter-writing economy. When we send each other (our selves as other) messages that we "are" men or women, our messages are often misread, delayed, not delivered. But the possibility of interrupted delivery means that we can transmit our selves in different ways. If letters tell us who we are, we are in words which consistently tell on us. These moments of destabilized sexual identity de/scribe the *différance* within "woman," within subjectivity, and inscribe identity—including sexual identity—as a process, a vacillation.

Kroetsch's texts are undelivered, undeliverable "letters." To read Kroetsch's texts "as a feminist" is to engage in a kind of feminist work which challenges assumptions about the difference *between* men's and women's writing. If my reading of Kroetsch's texts tells the difference between men's and women's writing, it is only to say that language always tells on itself, signifies other than what it says, always sends itself to places we do not intend. If texts are sites of contradiction where differences within are told, the concepts of men and women as essentially different are called into question.

This feminist theory of subjectivity locates moments at which a(-)woman speaks and so finds its texts at any period in history, (un)signed by any "one," and attends to the play of textuality as well as to the signature of the author. Consider, for example, the final scene in Shakespeare's *As You Like It*. The boy actor playing the "woman" Rosalind playing at being a boy speaks and s/he says:

> *If I were a woman* I would kiss as many of you as had beards that pleas'd me, complexions that lik'd me, and breaths that I defied not; and I am sure, as many as have good beards, or good faces, or sweet breaths, will for my kind offer, when I make curtsy, bid me farewell. (400; italics added)

Who says "If I were a woman?" Does the "I" speak as a woman *or* as a man? S/he—the destabilized pronoun is entirely appropriate here—speaks as both and neither.

Consider now the similar shifts in the reader's (Jeremy's) assumptions about a "beautiful blonde" in the following scene from *Gone Indian*:

> So help me God I am sober and sane, she takes off her tattered mink coat.
>
> And her tattered red sweatshirt with its motto: Whatsoever is Truth.
>
> And her snowboots.
>
> And her old-fashioned patriotic plaid skirt, the Maple Leaf Tartan yet, one of the authorities observes.
>
> And then she takes off her tits.
>
> You heard me, Professor. Her sculpted and aerodynamic tits. And then she takes off her gold bracelet and her skirt-petticoat and her jockey shorts.

> Maybe the cock and balls are fake too, I don't know. This is a peculiar land, Professor. Illusion is rife. (8)

Like Demeter LePage, like Anna Dawe, "s/he" is in an ex/position, a position that is not that of a unified gendered subject. S/he assumes a series of positions according to the "clothes" she puts on, and takes off.

Throughout this book I have argued that we can reread the concept of "woman" by locating moments at which (sexual) identity breaks down, when messages are not delivered, at which meaning and speaking—sexual and otherwise—are carried out in the play of *différance*. As Derrida writes in *The Post Card*,

> As soon as there is, there is *différance* . . . , and there is postal manoeuvering, relays, delay, anticipation, destination, telecommunicating network, the possibility, and therefore the fatal necessity of going astray. (66)

Just as Derrida's project, in *The Post Card*, is to point out the impossibilities of sending meaning—he wants an epistemological shift in our understanding of the workings of the postal structure—so, too, Kroetsch insists that we treat identity—speaking as men or as women—as that which "posits or posts itself otherwise" (66).

In the post-postal era, Derrida suggests, and Kroetsch's texts corroborate, the possibility,

> of a communications network without "destiny" or "destination," in which mail (messages) would be addressed only "to whom it may concern"—a system which values "noise" or invention over transparent meanings. Moreover, he [Derrida] shows us the writing which is appropriate for such an era: "It suffices to manipulate," he says, referring to the model post card, "to cut out, glue, and set going or parcel out, with hidden displacements and great tropic agility" [*Carte Postale* 21]. (Ulmer, "The Object of Post-Criticism" 107)

Kroetsch's work can be read as abandoning the conventions, not only of realism, but of realist criticism which assume that "one" can set up a direct "correspondence" between the object of study and the criticism produced. Kroetsch's texts ask us to, as Kristeva says, "labour in language" and to recognize the ways that all we *can* say is "*I can't tell*" (*The Post Card* 47). As I do, Derrida likes "that expression, because of the sonority, and all the meanings that resonate together in it: to count, to recount, to guess, to say, to discern. For us, for our future, *nobody* can tell'' (47). But ''to tell you'' is, for Derrida and for Kroetsch, ''all'' and ''it will have to hold on snapshot post cards—and immediately be divided among them. Letters in small pieces, torn in advance, cut out, recut'' (22).

What the postal institution—based, as it is, on the necessity of sending letters, or corresponding—''cannot bear is,'' in Derrida's words, ''for anyone to tamper with language. . . . It can bear more readily the most apparently revolutionary ideological sorts of 'content,' if only that content does not touch the borders of language and of all the juridico-political contracts it guarantees'' (''Living On: Borderlines'' 94-95). Subversively, Kroetsch's texts tamper with language, offering

> etymologies
> of sun or
> stone of ear
> and listening
>
> the bent of
> birth on edge
> the chrysalis
> and parting bone
>
> old as old as
> time as time
> holding
> hand of hand
>
> *hearing*
> *footfalls*
> *that must*
> *be those*
> *of a bear*
>
> ('' 'Morning, Jasper Park' '' from
> *The Criminal Intensities of Love*
> *as Paradise* in *Field Notes* 137)

Kroetsch's texts are writings in a post-postal era without a single message to be sent: ''And when the stranger came to my shore, he, my father, was that stranger. There are no truths, only correspondences'' (*Badlands* 45). Kroetsch's texts ''send us off,'' but only to (b)other texts.

Kroetsch's texts are, in Ulmer's phrase, "objects of post-criticism." The post-critic's job is to "explore the literal-letteral—level of language," a

> horizontal investigation of the polysemous meaning simultaneously available in the words themselves—in etymologies and puns—and in the things the words name. ("The Object of Post-Criticism" 95)

Kroetsch's texts are what Maureen Quilligan calls "narrative allegories" (30) which "favor the material of the signifier over the meanings of the signifieds" (Ulmer, "The Object of Post-Criticism" 95).

In/conclusion, I suggest that if there *is* a movement "beyond feminism," "my beyond" is, like Gregory Ulmer's in his argument for "post(e)-pedagogy," "really an 'elsewhere' or 'other than,' since I cannot pretend to surpass the work of my predecessors" (*Applied Grammatology* xiv). The work of my predecessors is inevitably the work with/in which I engage: "Post-critics write with the discourse of others (the already-written)" (Ulmer, "The Object of Post-Criticism" 96). With the discourse of others, I write now "to whom it may concern" these postscriptive dialogues in difference:

> Different though the sexes are, they intermix. In every human being a vacillation from one sex to the other takes place, and often it is only the clothes that keep the male or female likeness, while underneath the sex is the very opposite of what it is above.
>
> —Woolf, *Orlando*

> In "woman" I see something that cannot be represented, something that is not said, something above and beyond nomenclatures and ideologies. There are certain "men" who are familiar with this phenomenon; it is what some modern texts never stop signifying: testing the limits of language and sociality—the law and its transgression, mastery and (sexual) pleasure—without reserving one for males and the other for females. . . . From this point of view, it seems that certain feminist demands revive a kind of naive romanticism, a belief in identity.
>
> —Kristeva, "Woman Can Never Be Defined" in Marks and De Courtivron

Women need not take up with mean things since *they* are capable of the best. . . . The cause therefore of the defects *we* labour under is, if not wholly, yet at least in the first place, to be ascribed to the mistakes of *our* education, which like an error in the first concoction, spreads its ill influence through all *our* lives. . . . *Women* are from *their* very infancy debarred those advantages, with the want of which *they* are afterwards reproached, and nursed up in those vices which will hereafter be upbraided to *them.*

– Astell; italics added

The fact that, if I speak these words, a woman and a-woman, those who hear them cannot tell the difference . . . may convey two points I've tried to make: first, the potential of employing grammar and rhetoric in mutually subverting support, in support of subversive narrative practices; and second, the contradiction in which I find myself, as I speak, and which I am at pains to articulate here in writing.

– de Lauretis, *Technologies of Gender*

Bibliography

Bibliography

A Special Tribute to Robert Kroetsch. Prairie Fire 8.4 (1987-88).

Abel, Elizabeth, guest ed. "Writing and Sexual Difference." *Critical Inquiry* 8.2 (1981): 173-402.

"A Canadian Issue." *Boundary 2* 3.1 (1974).

Althusser, Louis. "Ideology and Ideological State Apparatuses (Notes towards an Investigation)." *Lenin and Philosophy and Other Essays*, pp. 127-86. Trans. Ben Brewster. London: New Left Books, 1971.

Ariès, Philippe, and André Béjin, eds. *Western Sexuality: Practice and Precept in Past and Present Times*. Oxford: Oxford Univ. Press, 1985.

Astell, Mary. *A Serious Proposal to the Ladies. Before Their Time: Six Women Writers of the Eighteenth Century*, pp. 28-47. Ed. Katharine M. Rogers. New York: Frederick Ungar, 1979.

Atherton, Stanley S. "On Strategies," Review of Robert Kroetsch and Reingard M. Nischik, *Gaining Ground: European Critics on Canadian Literature*. *Canadian Literature* 115 (Winter 1987): 184-86.

Bal, Mieke. *Narratology: Introduction to the Theory of Narrative*. Trans. C. Van Boheeman. Toronto: Univ. of Toronto Press, 1985.

Barbour, Douglas. "Introduction" to Kroetsch's *The "Crow" Journals*, pp. 5-10. Edmonton: NeWest Press, 1980.

Barth, John. "The Literature of Exhaustion." *Atlantic* 2 (1967): 29-34.

Barthes, Roland. "The Death of the Author." *Image-Music-Text*. New York: Hill and Wang, 1977.

__________. *Roland Barthes by Roland Barthes*. Trans. Richard Howard. New York: The Noonday Press, 1977.

Beckett, Samuel. *Three Novels: Malloy, Malone Dies, The Unnameable*. Trans. Patrick Bowles. New York: Grove Press, 1958.

Bell, Daniel. *The Coming of Post-Industrial Society*. New York: Basic Books, 1973.

Belsey, Catherine. *Critical Practice*. London: Methuen, 1980.

__________. *The Subject of Tragedy: Identity and Difference in Renaissance Drama*. London: Methuen, 1985.

Benjamin, Walter. "The Task of the Translator." *Illuminations*, pp. 69-82. Ed. and intr. Hannah Arendt. Trans. Harry Zohn. New York: Schocken Books, 1969.

Blodgett, Edward D. "European Theory and Canadian Criticism." *Zeitschrift der Gesellschaft für Kanada-Studien* 6.2 (1986): 5-15.

Bowering, George. "The Painted Window: Notes on Post-Realist Fiction." *University of Windsor Review* 13.2 (1978): 24-36.

_________. "Stone Hammer Narrative." *Open Letter* 6.2-3 (1985): 131-44.

Bowie, Malcolm. *Freud, Proust and Lacan: Theory as Fiction.* New York: Cambridge Univ. Press, 1987.

Brossard, Nicole. *These Our Mothers Or, The Disintegrating Chapter.* Trans. Barbara Godard. Toronto: Coach House Quebec Translations, 1983.

Brown, Russell M., and Donna A. Bennett. "Magnus Eisengrim: The Shadow of the Trickster in the Novels of Robertson Davies." *Modern Fiction Studies* 22 (1976): 348-57.

Bruss, Elizabeth W. "Eye for I: Making and Unmaking Autobiography in Film." *Autobiography: Essays Theoretical and Critical*, pp. 296-320. Ed. James Olney. Princeton: Princeton Univ. Press, 1980.

Burke, Kenneth. *A Grammar of Motives.* Berkeley: Univ. of California Press, 1945.

Butler, Judith. *Gender Trouble: Feminism and the Subversion of Identity.* New York: Routledge, 1990.

Cameron, Barry. "Lacan: Implications of Psychoanalysis and Canadian Discourse." *Future Indicative: Literary Theory and Canadian Literature*, pp. 137-51. Ed. John Moss. Ottawa: University of Ottawa Press, 1987.

Caplan, Pat, ed. *The Cultural Construction of Sexuality.* London: Tavistock Publications, 1987.

Carroll, David. *The Subject in Question: The Languages of Theory and the Strategies of Fiction.* Chicago: Univ. of Chicago Press, 1982.

Cixous, Hélène. "The Laugh of the Medusa." *The* Signs *Reader: Women, Gender & Scholarship*, pp. 279-97. Ed. Elizabeth Abel and Emily K. Abel. Chicago: Univ. of Chicago Press, 1983.

Cohen, Ed. "Writing Gone Wilde: Homoerotic Desire in the Closet of Representation." *PMLA* 102.5 (1987): 801-13.

Coleridge, Samuel Taylor. "To William Wordsworth." *English Romantic Writers*, p. 436. Ed. David Perkins. New York: Harcourt Brace Jovanovich Inc., 1967.

Costello, Bonnie. "The 'Feminine' Language of Marianne Moore." *Women and Language in Literature and Society*, pp. 222-38. Ed. Sally McConnell-Ginet et al. New York: Praeger, 1980.

Coward, Rosalind. *Female Desire: Women's Sexuality Today.* London: Granada Publishing, 1984.

_________. *Patriarchal Precedents: Sexuality and Social Relations.* London: Routledge and Kegan Paul, 1983.

Culler, Jonathan. *On Deconstruction: Theory and Criticism after Structuralism.* Ithaca: Cornell Univ. Press, 1982.

Davey, Frank. "Introduction." *Open Letter* 5.4 (1983): 7-10.

_________. *Reading Canadian Reading.* Winnipeg: Turnstone, 1988.

Davidson, Arnold E. "History, Myth and Time in Robert Kroetsch's *Badlands.*" *Studies in Canadian Literature* 5 (1980): 127-37.

Davidson, Arnold I. "Sex and the Emergence of Sexuality." *Critical Inquiry* 14.1 (Autumn 1987): 16-48.

de Lauretis, Teresa. *Alice Doesn't: Feminism, Semiotics, Cinema.* Bloomington: Indiana Univ. Press, 1984.

_________. *Technologies of Gender: Essays on Theory, Film, and Fiction.* Bloomington: Indiana Univ. Press, 1987.

de Saussure, Ferdinand. *Course in General Linguistics. Deconstruction in Context*, pp. 141-68. Ed. Mark C. Taylor. Chicago: Univ. of Chicago Press, 1986.

Derrida, Jacques. *La Carte Postale.* Paris: Flammarion, 1980.

_________. "Différance." *Margins of Philosophy*, pp. 3-27. Trans. Alan Bass. Chicago: Univ. of Chicago Press, 1982.

_________. *Dissemination.* Chicago: Univ. of Chicago Press, 1982.

_________. "Living On: Borderlines." *Deconstruction and Criticism.* Ed. Harold Bloom. New York: Seabury, 1979.

_________. "My Chances/*Mes Chances*: A Rendezvous with Some Epicurean Stereophonies." *Taking Chances: Derrida, Psychoanalysis and Literature*, pp. 1-32. Ed. Joseph H. Smith and William Kerrigan. Baltimore: Johns Hopkins Univ. Press, 1984.

_________. *Of Grammatology.* Trans. Gayatri Chakravorty Spivak. Baltimore: Johns Hopkins Univ. Press, 1976.

_________. *The Post Card: From Socrates to Freud and Beyond.* Trans. Alan Bass. Chicago: Univ. of Chicago Press, 1987.

_________. "Signature Event Context." *Margins of Philosophy*, pp. 307-30. Trans. Alan Bass. Chicago: Univ. of Chicago Press, 1982.

_________. *Signsponge.* Trans. Richard Rand. New York: Columbia Univ. Press, 1984.

_________. *Speech and Phenomena: And Other Essays on Husserl's Theory of Signs.* Trans. David B. Allison. Evanston: Northwestern Univ. Press, 1973.

_________. *Spurs.* Trans. Barbara Harlow. Chicago: Univ. of Chicago Press, 1979.

_________. "Telepathie." *Furor* (1981): 5-41.

_________. "Women in the Beehive: A Seminar with Jacques Derrida." *Men in Feminism*, pp. 189-203. Ed. Alice Jardine and Paul Smith. New York: Methuen, 1987.

_________. *Writing and Difference.* Trans. Alan Bass. Chicago: Univ. of Chicago Press, 1978.

_________, and Christie V. McDonald. "Choreographies." *Diacritics* 12 (1982): 66-76.

Dictionary of Psychology. New York: Dell, 1975.

Dinnerstein, Dorothy. *The Mermaid and the Minotaur: Sexual Arrangements and Human Malaise*. New York: Colophon, 1977.

Doane, Janice, and Devon Hodges. *Nostalgia and Sexual Difference: The Resistance to Contemporary Feminism*. New York: Methuen, 1987.

Easthope, Antony. *Poetry as Discourse*. London: Methuen, 1983.

Edwards, Brian. "Novelist as Trickster: The Magical Presence of G. G. Marquez in Robert Kroetsch's *What the Crow Said*." *Essays on Canadian Writing* 34 (1987): 92-110.

Eisenstein, Hester. *Contemporary Feminist Thought*. Boston: G. K. Hall, 1985.

_________, and Alice Jardine, eds. *The Future of Difference*. Boston: G. K. Hall, 1980.

Erickson, Jon. "The Language of Presence: Sound Poetry and Artaud." *Boundary 2* 15.1,2 (1985/86): 279-90.

Essays on Robert Kroetsch: Reflections. *Open Letter* 5.8-9 (1984).

Finn, Geraldine. "Beyond Either/Or: Postmodernism and the Politics of Feminism." Presented at the workshop on "Feminism, Critical Theory and the Canadian Legal System." June 4-7, 1988. Windsor University. Unpublished ts.

Fish, Stanley. *Is There a Text in This Class? The Authority of Interpretive Communities*. Cambridge, Mass: Harvard Univ. Press, 1980.

Fogel, Stan. "'I see England, I see France . . .' Robert Kroetsch's *Alibi*." *Studies in Canadian Literature* 9.2 (1984): 233-40.

Foster, Hal, ed. *The Anti-Aesthetic: Essays on Postmodern Culture*. Port Townsend, Washington: Bay Press, 1983.

Foucault, Michel. *The History of Sexuality*. Vol. 1: *An Introduction*. Trans. Robert Hurley. New York: Vintage Books, 1980.

_________. *Language, Counter-Memory, Practice: Selected Essays and Interviews*. Ed. Donald F. Bouchard. Trans. Donald F. Bouchard and Sherry Simon. Ithaca: Cornell Univ. Press, 1977.

Freud, Sigmund. "Female Sexuality." *Women and Analysis: Dialogues on Psychoanalytic Views of Feminity*, pp. 39-56. Ed. Jean Strouse. Boston: G. K. Hall, 1985.

_________. "Femininity." *Women and Analysis: Dialogues on Psychoanalytic Views of Feminity*, pp. 73-94. Ed. Jean Strouse. Boston: G. K. Hall, 1985.

Gallop, Jane. *The Daughter's Seduction: Feminism and Psychoanalysis*. Ithaca, NY: Cornell Univ. Press, 1982.

Garvin, Harry R., ed. *Romanticism, Modernism, Postmodernism*. Cranbury: Associate Univ. Press, 1980.

Gass, William. "in the heart of the heart of the country." *Anti-Story*, pp. 132-60. Ed. Philip Stevick. New York: Collier MacMillan, 1971.

Gibbs, Robert. *All This Night Long*. Fredericton: Fiddlehead Poetry Books, 1973.

Gilbert, Sandra M., and Susan Gubar. *The Madwoman in the Attic: The Woman Writer and the Nineteenth-Century Literary Imagination*. New Haven: Yale Univ. Press, 1984.

Giles, Howard, Philip Smith, Caroline Brown et al. "Women's Speech: The Voice of Feminism." *Woman and Language in Literature and Society*, pp. 150-56. Ed. Sally McConnell-Ginet et al. New York: Praeger, 1980.

Godard, Barbara. Letter to the author. 30 November 1987.

_________. "Other Fictions: Robert Kroetsch's Criticism." *Open Letter* 5.8-9 (1984): 5-21.

_________, ed. *Gynocritics/La Gynocritique: Feminist Approaches to Writing by Canadian and Québécoise Women*. Toronto: ECW Press, 1987.

Goldman, Emma. *The Traffic in Women and other essays on feminism*. Albion, CA: Times Change Press, 1970.

Graham, K. W. "Picaro as Messiah: Backstrom's Election in *The Words of My Roaring*." *Mosaic* 14.2 (1981): 177-86.

Greene, Gayle, and Coppelia Kahn. *Making a Difference: Feminist Literary Criticism*. London: Methuen, 1985.

Gunn, Janet Varner. *Autobiography: Toward a Poetics of Experience*. Philadelphia: Univ. of Pennsylvania Press, 1982.

Gunnars, Kristjana. "Meditation on a Snowy Morning: A Conversation with Robert Kroetsch." *Prairie Fire* 8.4 (1987-88): 54-67.

Harvey, Connie. "Tear-Glazed Vision of Laughter." *Essays on Canadian Writing* 11 (1978): 28-54.

Hassan, Ihab. *Paracriticisms*. Urbana: Univ. of Illinois Press, 1975.

_________. "The Question of Postmodernism." *Romanticism, Modernism, Postmodernism*, pp. 117-26. Ed. Harry R. Garvin. Cranbury: Associated Univ. Press, 1980.

Heath, Stephen. *Questions of Cinema*. Bloomington: Indiana Univ. Press, 1981.

_________. "Male Feminism." *Men in Feminism*, pp. 1-32. Ed. Alice Jardine and Paul Smith. New York: Methuen, 1987.

Heidegger, Martin. *Poetry, Language, Thought*. Trans. and intr. Albert Hofstadten. New York: Harper & Row, 1971.

Hjartarson, Paul. "Discourse of the Other." Review of Robert Kroetsch, *Advice to My Friends*. *Canadian Literature* 115 (Winter 1987): 135-38.

Hubbard, Ruth. "The Social Construction of Female Biology." *Ideas*. With Lister Sinclair. Prod. Robert Prowse. CBC Toronto. 15 November 1983.

Hutcheon, Linda. *A Poetics of Postmodernism: History, Theory, Fiction.* New York: Routledge, 1988.

———. *The Canadian Postmodern.* Toronto: Oxford Univ. Press, 1988.

———. "Challenging the Conventions of Realism: Postmodernism in Canadian Literature." *The Canadian Forum* 66.758 (1986): 34-38.

———. "Beginning to Theorize Postmodernism." *Textual Practice* 1.1 (1987): 10-31.

———. *The Politics of Postmodernism.* New York: Routledge, 1989.

———. Review of *No Fixed Address: An Amorous Journey* by Aritha van Herk. *Dandelion* 15.1 (1988): 106-109.

———. "Subject in/of/to History and His Story." *Diacritics* 16.1 (1986): 78-91.

Irigaray, Luce. *This Sex Which Is Not One.* Trans. Catherine Porter. Ithaca: Cornell Univ. Press, 1977.

Jacobus, Mary. *Reading Woman: Essays in Feminist Criticism.* New York: Columbia Univ. Press, 1986.

Jaggar, Alison M. *Feminist Politics and Human Nature.* Totowa, NJ: Rowman and Allanheld, 1983.

Jamal, Ashraf Ali. "A Writing of Dangerous Middles: Reading Robert Kroetsch's *Alibi.*" M.A. thesis. University of New Brunswick. April 1985.

Jardine, Alice. "Gynesis." *Diacritics* 12 (1982): 54-65.

———. "Men in Feminism: Odor di Uomo or Compagnons de Route?" *Men in Feminism*, pp. 54-61. Ed. Alice Jardine and Paul Smith. New York: Methuen, 1987.

———, and Paul Smith. *Men in Feminism.* New York: Methuen, 1987.

Johnson, Barbara. *The Critical Difference: Essays in the Contemporary Rhetoric of Reading.* Baltimore: Johns Hopkins Univ. Press, 1980.

———. *A World of Difference.* Baltimore: Johns Hopkins Univ. Press, 1987.

Johnson, Nora. Editorial Reply to Erica Jong. *The New York Times Book Review.* 24 April 1988, 49.

———. "Housewives and Prom Queens, 25 Years Later." *The New York Times Book Review.* 20 March 1988, 1, 32, 33.

Jones, Ann Rosalind. "Writing the Body: Toward an Understanding of l'Ecriture Feminine." *The New Feminist Criticism: Essays on Women, Literature and Theory*, pp. 361-77. Ed. Elaine Showalter. New York: Pantheon, 1985.

Jones, Manina. "Roses are Read." Review of Robert Kroetsch, *Excerpts from the Real World. Canadian Literature* 119 (Winter 1988): 119-23.

Jong, Erica. Editorial, "Housewives and Prom Queens." 24 April 1988, 49.

Jouvet, Jean, ed. *Magritte.* Genf: Cosmopress, 1982.

Kamboureli, Smaro. "A Poem *out of* Love: An Interview with Robert Kroetsch on *The Sad Phoenician*." *Open Letter* 5.8-9 (1984): 47-52.

Kristeva, Julia. *Desire in Language: A Semiotic Approach to Literature and Art*. Ed. Leon S. Roudiez. Trans. Thomas Gora, Alice Jardine, Leon S. Roudiez. New York: Columbia Univ. Press, 1980.

__________. *Tales of Love*. Trans. Leon S. Roudiez. New York: Columbia Univ. Press, 1987.

__________. "Women's Time." *Feminist Theory: A Critique of Ideology*. Trans. Alice Jardine and Harry Blake. Ed. Nannerl O. Kerohane et al. Chicago: Univ. of Chicago Press, 1981.

Kroetsch, Robert. *Advice to My Friends*. Don Mills, Ontario: Stoddart, 1985.

__________. *Alberta*. Toronto: Macmillan, 1962.

__________. *Alibi*. Don Mills, Ontario: Stoddart, 1985.

__________. *Badlands*. Toronto: New Press, 1975.

__________. "Beyond Nationalism: A Prologue." *Open Letter* 5.4 (1983): 83-89.

__________. *But We Are Exiles*. Toronto: Macmillan, 1965.

__________. "Canada is a Poem." *Open Letter* 5.4 (1983): 33-35.

__________. "The Canadian Writer and the American Literary Tradition." *Open Letter* 5.4 (1983): 11-15.

__________. "Carnival and Violence: A Meditation." *Open Letter* 5.4 (1983): 111-22.

__________. *Completed Field Notes: The Long Poems of Robert Kroetsch*. Toronto: McClelland & Stewart, 1989.

__________. "Contemporary Standards in the Canadian Novel." *Open Letter* 5.4 (1983): 37-46.

__________. "The Continuing Poem." *Open Letter* 5.4 (1983): 81-82.

__________, ed. *Creation*. With James Bacque and Pierre Gravel. Toronto: New Press, 1970.

__________. *The "Crow" Journals*. Edmonton: NeWest Press, 1980.

__________. "Delphi: Commentary." *Open Letter* 5.8-9 (1984): 22-40.

__________. "The Disappearing Father and Harrison's Born Again and Again and Again West." *Essays on Canadian Writing* 11 (1978): 7-9.

__________. "Effing the Ineffable." *Open Letter* 5.4 (1983): 23-24.

__________. *Excerpts from the Real World*. Lantzville, B.C.: Oolichan Books, 1986.

__________. "The Exploding Porcupine: Violence of Form in English-Canadian Fiction." *Open Letter* 5.4 (1983): 57-64.

__________. "The Fear of Women in Prairie Fiction." *Open Letter* 5.4 (1983): 47-55.

__________. *Field Notes 1-8 a Continuing Poem: The Collected Poetry of Robert Kroetsch*. Don Mills, Ontario: General, 1981.

_________. "For Play and Entrance." *Open Letter* 5.4 (1983): 91-110.
_________. *Gone Indian.* Toronto: New Press, 1973.
_________. "Grammar of Silence: Narrative Pattern in Ethnic Writing." *Canadian Literature* 106 (1985): 65-74.
_________. *The Lovely Treachery of Words: Essays Selected and New.* Toronto: Oxford Univ. Press, 1989.
_________. *The Ledger.* London, Ontario: Applegarth Follies, 1975.
_________. "On Being an Alberta Writer." *Open Letter* 5.4 (1983): 69-80.
_________. *The Sad Phoenician.* Toronto: Coach House Press, 1979.
_________. *Seed Catalogue.* Winnipeg: Turnstone, 1977.
_________. *Seed Catalogue.* (With "Spending the Morning on the Beach.") Winnipeg: Turnstone Press, 1986.
_________. *The Stone Hammer Poems: 1960-1975.* Nanaimo, B.C.: Oolichan Books, 1975.
_________. *The Studhorse Man.* Toronto: Macmillan, 1969.
_________. "Taking the Risk." *Open Letter* 5.4 (1983): 65-67.
_________. *What the Crow Said.* Don Mills, Ontario: General Publishing, 1978.
_________. *The Words of My Roaring.* London: Macmillan, 1966.
_________, and Reingard M. Nischik, eds. *Gaining Ground: European Critics on Canadian Literature.* Edmonton: NeWest Press, 1985.
Krupnick, Mark. *Displacement: Derrida and After.* Bloomington: Indiana Univ. Press, 1983.
Lacan, Jacques. "The Agency of the Letter in the Unconscious or Reason Since Freud." *Ecrits: A Selection*, pp. 146-75. Trans. Alan Sheridan. New York: W. W. Norton, 1977.
_________. *Speech and Language in Psychoanalysis.* Trans. Anthony Wilden. Baltimore: Johns Hopkins Univ. Press, 1968.
Lakoff, Robin. *Language and Women's Place.* New York: Harper & Row, 1975.
Lecker, Robert. *Robert Kroetsch.* Boston: Twayne Publisher, 1986.
Lentricchia, Frank. "Anatomy of a Jar." *The South Atlantic Quarterly* 86.4 (1987): 397-402.
_________. *Criticism and Social Change.* Chicago: Univ. of Chicago Press, 1983.
MacKendrick, Louis K. "Robert Kroetsch and the Modern Canadian Novel of Exhaustion." *Essays on Canadian Writing* 11 (1978): 10-27.
Macksey R., and E. Donato, eds. *The Language of Criticism and the Sciences of Man.* Baltimore: Johns Hopkins Univ. Press, 1970. (Derrida's "Structure, Sign, and Play in the Discourse of the Human Sciences" appears here – pp. 242-72 – and in *Writing and Difference.*)
Mandel, Ann. "Robert Kroetsch: Rara Avis: A Review of Kroetsch's Critical Essays." *Open Letter* 5.8-9 (1984): 53-56.
Mandel, Eli. *The Family Romance.* Winnipeg: Turnstone Press, 1986.

________. "Introduction" to *Field Notes*, 5-8.

Marks, Elaine, and Isabelle de Courtivron, eds. *New French Feminisms: An Anthology*. Amherst: Univ. of Massachusetts Press, 1980.

Mayne, Judith. "Feminist Film Theory and Women at the Movies." *Profession* 87. 14-19.

McConnell-Ginet, Sally, Ruth Borker, Nelly Furman, eds. *Women and Language in Literature and Society*. New York: Praeger, 1980.

McCormick, Kathleen, Gary Waller, and Linda Flower. *Reading Texts: Reading, Responding, Writing*. Lexington, MA: D.C. Heath and Company, 1987.

Meese, Elizabeth. *Crossing the Double Cross: The Practice of Feminist Theory*. Chapel Hill: Univ. of North Carolina Press, 1986.

Mitchell, Juliet, and Jacqueline Rose, eds. *Feminine Sexuality: Jacques Lacan and the école freudienne*. Trans. Jacqueline Rose. New York: Pantheon, 1982.

Moi, Toril. *Sexual/Textual Politics*. London: Methuen, 1985.

________, ed. *The Kristeva Reader*. New York: Columbia Univ. Press, 1986.

Moss, John, ed. *Future Indicative: Literary Theory and Canadian Literature*. Ottawa: Univ. of Ottawa Press, 1987.

Munich, Adrienne. "Notorious Signs: Feminist Criticism and Literary Tradition." *Making a Difference: Feminist Literary Criticism*, pp. 238-59. Ed. Gayle Greene and Coppelia Kahn. London: Methuen, 1985.

Neuman, Shirley. "Allow Self, Portraying Self: Autobiography in *Field Notes*." *Line* 2 (1983): 104-21.

________. "Figuring the Reader, Figuring the Self in Field Notes: 'Double or Noting.'" *Open Letter*. 5.8-9 (Summer-Fall 1984): 176-94.

________. "Unearthing Language: An Interview with Rudy Wiebe and Robert Kroetsch." *A Voice in the Land: Essays By and About Rudy Wiebe*. Ed. W. J. Keith. Edmonton: NeWest Press, 1981.

________, and Smaro Kamboureli, eds. *A Mazing Space: Writing Canadian Women Writing*. Edmonton: NeWest Press,

________, and Robert Wilson, eds. *Labyrinths of Voice: Conversations with Robert Kroetsch*. Edmonton: NeWest Press, 1982. 1986.

Nichol, bp. "The Lungs: A Draft" (from *Autobiography*). *Now*. Literary Supplement. 31 March - 6 April 1988, 45.

Nicholson, Linda J., ed. *Feminism/Postmodernism*. New York: Routledge, 1990.

Nicolaisen, W. F. H. "Ordering the Chaos: Name Strategies in Robert Kroetsch's Novels." *Essays on Canadian Writing* 11 (1978): 55-65.

Norris, Christopher. *Deconstruction: Theory and Practice*. New York: Methuen, 1982.

Nyquist, Mary, and Margaret W. Ferguson, eds. *Re-Membering Milton: Essays on the Texts and Traditions*. New York: Methuen, 1987.

O'Brien, Mary. *The Politics of Reproduction.* Boston: Routledge & Kegan Paul, 1981.

Olney, James. "Autobiography and the Cultural Moment: A Thematic, Historical, and Bibliographical Introduction." *Autobiography: Essays Theoretical and Critical*, pp. 3-27. Ed. James Olney. Princeton: Princeton Univ. Press, 1980.

________, ed. *Autobiography: Essays Theoretical and Critical.* Princeton: Princeton Univ. Press, 1980.

Ondaatje, Michael. *The Long Poem Anthology.* Toronto: Coach House Press, 1979.

Ortner, Sherry B. "Is Female to Male as Nature is to Culture?" *Woman, Culture, and Society*, pp. 67-87. Ed. Michelle Zimbalist Rosaldo and Louise Lamphere. Stanford: Stanford Univ. Press, 1974.

Poirier, Richard. "Writing Off the Self." *Raritan* 1.1 (1981): 106-33.

Quilligan, Maureen. *The Language of Allegory.* Ithaca: Cornell Univ. Press, 1979.

Ricou, Laurie. "Phyllis Webb, Daphne Marlatt and Simultitude." *A Mazing Space: Writing Canadian Women Writing*, pp. 205-15. Ed. Shirley Neuman and Smaro Kamboureli. Edmonton: NeWest Press, 1986.

Rimmon-Kenan, Shlomith. *Narrative Fiction: Contemporary Poetics.* New York: Methuen, 1983.

Robert Kroetsch: Essays. Ed. Frank Davey and bp Nichol. *Open Letter* 5.4 (1983).

The Robert Kroetsch Papers: First Accession. Calgary: Univ. of Calgary Press, 1986.

Ross, Morton L. "Robert Kroetsch and His Novels." *Writers of the Prairies*, pp. 101-14. Ed. Donald G. Stephens. Vancouver: Univ. of British Columbia Press, 1973.

Rudy Dorscht, Susan. "A Deconstructive Narratology: Reading Robert Kroetsch's *Alibi.*" *Open Letter* 6.8 (Summer 1987): 78-83.

________. "Blown Figures and Blood: Toward a Feminist/Poststructuralist Reading of Audrey Thomas' Writing." *Future Indicative: Literary Theory and Canadian Literature*, pp. 221-27. Ed. John Moss. Ottawa: Univ. of Ottawa Press, 1987.

________. "How *The Studhorse Man* Makes Love: A Postfeminist Analysis." *Canadian Literature* 119 (1988): 25-31.

________. "Telling the Difference: Rereading 'Woman,' with Robert Kroetsch's Writing." Ph.D. Dissertation. York University. June 1988.

Ruthven, K. K. *Feminist Literary Studies: An Introduction.* Cambridge: Cambridge Univ. Press, 1984.

Ryan, Michael. *Marxism and Deconstruction: A Critical Articulation.* Baltimore: Johns Hopkins Univ. Press, 1982.

Said, Edward. "An Ethics of Language." *Diacritics* 4.2 (Summer 1974).

Scholes, Robert. "Reading Like a Man." *Men in Feminism*, pp. 204-18. Ed. Alice Jardine and Paul Smith. New York: Methuen, 1987.

_________. *Textual Power: Literary Theory and the Teaching of English*. New Haven: Yale Univ. Press, 1985.

Seim, Jeanette. "Horses and Houses: Further Readings in Kroetsch's *Badlands* and Sinclair Ross's *As For Me and My House*." *Open Letter* 5.8-9 (1984): 94-115.

Shakespeare, William. *As You Like It. The Riverside Shakespeare*, pp. 365-402. Ed. G. Blakemore Evans et al. London: Houghton Mifflin, 1974.

Showalter, Elaine. *A Literature of Their Own: British Women Novelists from Bronte to Lessing*. London: Virage Press, 1978.

_________. "Feminist Criticism in the Wilderness." *Critical Inquiry* 8.2 (Winter 1981): 179-205.

_________, ed. *The New Feminist Criticism: Essays on Women, Literature and Theory*. New York: Pantheon, 1985.

Silverman, Kaja. *The Subject of Semiotics*. New York: Oxford Univ. Press, 1983.

Smith, Joseph H., and William Kerrigan, eds. *Taking Chances: Derrida, Psychoanalysis and Literature*. Baltimore: Johns Hopkins Univ. Press, 1984.

Smith, Paul. *Discerning the Subject*. Minneapolis: Univ. of Minnesota Press, 1988.

Smith, Sidonie. *A Poetics of Women's Autobiography: Marginality and the Fictions of Self-Representation*. Bloomington: Indiana Univ. Press, 1987.

Sontag, Susan. *Against Interpretation*. New York: Noonday Press, 1961.

Spivak, Gayatri Chakravorty. "Displacement and the Discourse of Woman." *Displacement: Derrida and After*, pp. 169-95. Ed. Mark Krupnick. Bloomington: Indiana Univ. Press, 1983.

Sprinker, Michael "Fictions of the Self: The End of Autobiography." *Autobiography: Essays Theoretical and Critical*, pp. 321-42. Ed. James Olney. Princeton: Princeton Univ. Press, 1980.

Stanzel, Franz K. "Texts Recycled: 'Found' Poems Found in Canada." *Gaining Ground: European Critics on Canadian Literature*, pp. 91-106. Ed. Robert Kroetsch, Reingard M. Nischik. Edmonton: NeWest Press, 1985.

Stasio, Marilyn. "The Feminist Movement: Where We Stand Today." *Cosmopolitan*. 262-65. May 1988.

Stein, Gertrude. *Lectures in America*. New York: Random House, 1935.

_________. *Tender Buttons. Selected Writings of Gertrude Stein*, p. 474. Ed. Carl Van Bechten. New York: Vintage Books, 1962.

Stoller, Robert J. "Facts and Fancies: An Examination of Freud's Concept of Bisexuality." *Women and Analysis: Dialogues on Psychoana-*

lytic Views of Feminity, pp. 343-64. Ed. Jean Strouse. Boston: G. K. Hall, 1985.
Strouse, Jean, ed. *Woman and Analysis: Dialogues on Psychoanalytic Views of Femininity*. Boston: G. K. Hall, 1985.
Sullivan, Rosemary. "The Fascinating Place Between: The Fiction of Robert Kroetsch." *Mosaic* 11.3 (Spring 1978): 165-76.
Surette, P. L. "The Fabular Fiction of Robert Kroetsch." *Canadian Literature* 77 (1978): 6-19.
Taylor, Mark C. *Deconstruction in Context*. Chicago: Univ. of Chicago Press, 1986.
Thomas, Peter. *Robert Kroetsch*. Vancouver: Douglas and McIntyre, 1980.
Todd, Janet. *Feminist Literary History*. New York: Routledge, 1988.
Tostevin, Lola Lemire. *'sophie*. Toronto: Coach House Press, 1988.
Turner, M. E. "Canadian Literature and Robert Kroetsch: A Case of Canonization." *Dalhousie Review* 67.1 (1987): 56-72.
Ulmer, Gregory. *Applied Grammatology: Post(e)-Pedagogy from Jacques Derrida to Joseph Beuys*. Baltimore: Johns Hopkins Univ. Press, 1985.
_________. "The Object of Post-Criticism." *The Anti-Aesthetic: Essays on Postmodern Culture*. Ed. Hal Foster. Port Townsend, WA: Bay Press, 1983.
_________. "The Post-Age." *Diacritics* 11 (1981): 39-56.
van Herk, Aritha. "Biocritical Essay." *The Robert Kroetsch Papers: First Accession*. Calgary: Univ. of Calgary Press, 1986.
_________. *No Fixed Address: An Amorous Journey*. Toronto: McClelland & Stewart, 1986.
_________. "(no parrot/no crow/no parrot)." *Prairie Fire* 8.4 (1987-88): 12-20.
_________. Review of *The Lovely Treachery of Words*. *The Globe and Mail*. 15 April 1989.
Waller, Gary F. "Deconstruction and Renaissance Literature." *Assays: Critical Approaches to Medieval and Renaissance Texts*. Vol. 2, pp. 69-93. Ed. Peggy A. Knapp. Pittsburgh: Univ. of Pittsburgh Press, 1983.
_________. "I and Ideology: Demystifying the Self of Contemporary Poetry." *Denver Quarterly* 18.3 (1983): 123-38.
Weed, Elizabeth, ed. *Coming to Terms: Feminism, Theory, Politics*. New York: Routledge, 1989.
Weedon, Chris. *Feminist Practice and Poststructuralist Theory*. Oxford: Basil Blackwell, 1987.
Wood, Susan. "Reinventing the Word: Robert Kroetsch's Poetry." *Canadian Literature* 77 (1978): 28-39.
Woolf, Virginia. *Orlando*. London: Hogarth Press, 1928.
Wright, Elizabeth. *Psychoanalytic Criticism*. London: Methuen, 1984.

Index

Index